Programming Constructs in JAVA

by

Sarthak Saxena

(University of petroleum and energy studies, dehradun)

PARTRIDGE

A Penguin Random House Company

To order additional copies of this book, contact
Partridge India
000 800 10062 62
www.partridgepublishing.com/india
orders.india@partridgepublishing.com

CONTENTS

Dedicated to my parents, jiju
and my lovely sister

PREFACE

Programming Constructs In Java has been created with the objective to empower the reader to make a firm footing in the programming world by chiefly focussing on the basics and steadily working upon brainstorming program constructions. We believe if the foundation of a building is strong, then it is strong enough to hold a magnanimous structure. Similarly, this book has dived into the depths of the concepts for its pursuers. The book is provided with numerous examples from the very basic levels to highly advanced standards. The conceptualization and visualization of the book has incorporated the best ways to keep the reader glued till the very end. The author, a computer engineer, techie and a student himself, has assimilated all his knowledge absorbed over these years and nurtured this project. Utmost care has been taken while explaining a concept to make it crystal clear to students of all levels. Every topic has been dealt with perfection in the most simple and easy to understand language. The tenacious topics in programming require profound scrutiny to acquire complete knowledge. Hence, umpteen examples have been used for topics like **Arrays, Strings, and Data Structure** to ensure the users have a firm grip on them. All the examples ascertain the simplicity and precision as per the demand, also the compiled programs are absolutely genuine, for they have been run and debugged personally. Run through it and be a master Programmer in Java. Happy Readings!

ACKNOWLEDGEMENT

Many pearls harmonize to form a necklace; likewise this book is not entirely the work of one person. I owe a debt of gratitude to all and sundry who patiently scrutinized the manuscript and gave valuable suggestions, of which I took advantage of and made some additions.

The sole credit of this whole idea of creating a user friendly book on programming was injected into me by my mother **Dr. Amita Saxena**, her keen insight observed my intense passion and excellence in the subject. Being a professor herself she has convincingly inflamed the idea from a feeble spark into a mighty blaze. I am grateful to her for the never ending support and guidance.

I would like to extend my heartfelt gratitude to the faculty of my university, **Mr. G. Hanumat Shashtry** for his dexterous, ingenious and far-reaching masters of the subject, for his advice and cooperation during the advancement of the project. I record my gratitude to my sister **Ms. Kriti** and my friend **Akash Raj**, whose constant motivational reinforcement and critical comment have been a source of great encouragement. I would also like to thank **Deepankar Agarwal** for the interior and cover designing of the book. This book is would never have been completed without their help.

SPECIAL THANKS

Dipika Chatterje completed her schooling from St. Mary's Convent Inter College, Lucknow, in the year 2013. She has a keen interest in computer programming. After being introduced to the amazing JAVA language in class VIII, she has excelled in the language. She holds a great command in programming and thus is pursuing her further studies in computer applications, and doing BCA(Bachelor of Computer Applications).

She has helped me in various complications of the book. I could have never compiled it without her help. I would just like to thank her for all the help and motivation.

CHAPTER 1

BASIC PROGRAMMING

- Introductory Theory
- Basic Concepts of Java
- Programs
- Program Notes
- Practice Questions
- Short-answer Questions
- Multiple-choice Questions

1

Programs At a Glance

➤ Program to print 'Java is wonderful'.
➤ Program to add two numbers.
➤ Program to input two numbers from the user and then add them.
➤ Program to input two float numbers and perform basic mathematical operations on them.
➤ Program to enter three numbers and find their average.
➤ Program to print:

```
* * * * * * *
*           *
* * * * * * *
```

➤ Program to calculate the simple interest.
➤ Program to calculate the area of a triangle.
➤ Program to find the distance between two coordinate points.
➤ Program to calculate the compound interest on a given set of rate principle and amount.
➤ Program to enter the temperature of a city in Fahrenheit and convert it into Centigrade.
➤ Program to enter two numbers and swap their values.
➤ Program to enter two numbers and swap them without using any third variable.
➤ Program to enter the marks in five subjects of a student and then calculate his percentage.
➤ Program to find the area of a circle.
➤ Program to enter the basic salary of an employee and then calculate his gross salary.
➤ Program to generate a random number in java.
➤ Program to print the total bill of the customer.
➤ Program to input a character and print its ASCII value.
➤ Program to input a character in upper case and print it in lower case.
➤ Program to enter the distance in km and convert it into metres, centimetres, milimetres.

1.1 INTRODUCTION

To begin your encounter with the subject it is mandatory to clear your basic concepts. Therefore, the following chapter has been designed to cater your requirements for understanding the basics clearly. A number of illustrations and programs have been provided along with. Some useful notes have been provided along with the program to so that you get the knowledge of some of the key points clearly.

It is also advised that you solve the practice questions given along with the solved programs so that the way and the concepts of programming are clear to you. So let us begin with the key concepts of programming. We all know that java is a programming language, but before going through the basics let's see what a **program** is and what do we actually mean by a **programming language.**

1.2 WHAT ARE PROGRAMS?

Prior to getting into technicality first examine your daily schedule. Daily you to a series of task one after the other like,

Wake up, get fresh
↓
Do breakfast and then go to school
↓
Attend the classes
↓
Go to evening coaching
↓
Play with friends
↓
Have Dinner, sleep

This is nothing but our schedule, our **program** for the day. Consider another example, in our day to day life we say that today I will go to school, then play football, then go for movie and finally have dinner. So in a way we are doing a number of things one after the other or step by step. Similarly a program is also a step by step execution of a number of statements.

In terms of Programming, A **program** is a set of instructions written to perform a particular operation. A program may be complex or simple but it should have the ability to use the input to generate a valid output.

In java we have two types of programs:

(i) Stand-alone applications

Standalone applications are those applications which run of the user's machine i.e. on command prompt or an IDE (Integrated Development Environment). It would take certain input and give a desired output.

(ii) Applets

An applet is a java program that runs on a java enabled web browser.

1.3 PROGRAMMING LANGUAGE

We all know that Java is a programming language. But what do we actually mean by saying 'language'. We can say that language is nothing but a medium of communication. Now consider the following scenario:

There is a person from India and another person from France. Now both of them don't know each other's language. So how do they communicate with each other? The problem is simple and so is the answer. We can have a mediator between those two persons who can translate the thing said by one person and convey it to the other person. So in this way that mediator enables the communication between them.

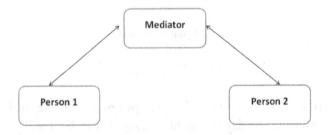

So in the same way when we talk of programming, the language which we write and understand is not understood by the system. So a compiler and interpreter are used to convert the **source code** (i.e. the code which we type) into **machine code** (i.e. the code that the machine understands).

A **compiler** is software which converts the source into written by the user into a machine readable and understandable code.

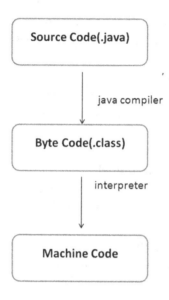

The code which is written by the user is termed as **source code.** Now this code is compiled by the java compiler and if no syntactical error is found the **byte code** is generated. The byte code is an intermediary code. The byte code is the same for all systems i.e. it is independent of the platform. Next, the byte code is interpreted by the interpreter and finally the **machine code** is obtained. The machine code is different for all platform and all systems.

1.4 FEATURES OF JAVA

If a particular language if ruling the world of programming then it must have some unique features. Java has a lot of them which make it so popular. A few have been listed below:

- **Simple**
The code written in java is simple and easy to understand. The syntax is easy as well as the programming concepts are easy to use and understand.

- **Robust**

The programs written in java are strong. They do not usually crash due to some uncontrollable reasons.

- **Secure**

Security is a major issue when it comes to programming. The programs written in java are highly secured from any external threats.

- **Platform Independent**

This is one of the main reasons why java is preferred over C and C++. The programs written in java can be executed on anywhere irrespective of the system.

- **Both compiled and interpreted**

The programs written in java are first compiled to generate the byte code and then this byte code is interpreted to generate the executable code.

- **Object-oriented programming**

Java offers us with a more real world programming experience with the concept of objects. Almost everything in java is an object.

- **Distributed**

Java is designed as a distributed language because of which developers and programs from remote locations and access both the data and programs and work in a collaborative manner

- **Performance**

The programs written in java are highly fast even though the language is interpreted. The execution time is quite less.

1.5 CONCEPT OF OBJECTS AND CLASSES

In real world objects are all around us. Everything that we see, use, etc. are all examples of objects. Eg: A Pen. Every object has some characteristics and shows a particular behavior. Eg: The characteristics of a pen are that is it cylindrical in shape, it has a cap at the top, etc. while its behavior is that it allows us to write.

Similarly in the programming world also objects exhibit some characteristics and behavior. Technically we can say that, **an object is an instance of a class.**

Now the next thing is what is a class? A class is a collection containing the objects which have some characteristics or behavior in common. Eg: Mobile, laptops, pen drive are all members of the class Gadgets. So, we can say that **a class is a blueprint for the creation of objects.** We can create as many objects as required when a class has been declared. An object operates upon the data and the methods of the class.

Now let us see this concept through an example.

```
class abc
{
    int a;
    public void geta()
    {
        // this method will input the value of a
    }
}
```

Now if we create two objects of class abc, **obj1 and obj2.** So, every object will access the data members and member methods of the class.

But, the objects don't share the data members i.e. every object will have its own separate copy of the data members. Any change in one object will not reflect in the other.

The syntax for creation of object is:

[class name] [object name]=new [class name]();

The new operator is used to allocate memory to the created object.

1.6 KEY CONCEPTS OF OOPS

Object-oriented programming is an advanced concept of programming. It has a variety of features and advantages. However the key concepts of OOPS include:

(i) Encapsulation

The binding up of data and functions into a single unit called class is called encapsulation. Because of this feature the data is only accessible to the functions inside the class i.e. the outside world cannot access it. This provides the facility of **data hiding.**

(ii) Abstraction

Representing only the essential features and hiding unnecessary details is called abstraction. Eg: When we board a plane, we are told only the basic instructions like how to use the seat belt, emergency doors, etc. but we are not told how to fly the aircraft because it's beyond our use. That is what abstraction does.

(iii) Inheritance

Inheritance basically means deriving the properties of one class into another class. The derived class is called the child class and the class whose properties are being derived is called the parent class. Inheritance helps in the reusability of the code. It has been explained later in chapter 11.

(iv) Polymorphism

Polymorphism means existence in more than one form. In java, polymorphism is implemented though function overloading and function overriding which have been explained in chapter 12.

1.7 TOKENS

Token is the smallest individual unit of a program. Eg: Consider the following statement:

int a=3;

So it is quite clear that each and every individual unit has a special purpose. Tokens are of various types:

(i) Keywords

To understand the concept of keywords, consider an Oxford dictionary. In the dictionary there are a number of words whose meaning have already been defined and we cannot change it.

Similarly, keywords are the words which convey a special meaning to the compiler. Their meaning cannot be changed throughout the program. Eg: int, class, if, etc. They cannot be used as names of variables because if we do so, we are trying to assign a new meaning to it which is not possible.

(ii) Identifiers

Identifiers are used for naming the different parts of the program like, the names of variables, literals, etc. There are certain rules which are needed to be followed:

(i) An identifier cannot be a keyword.
(ii) It cannot start with a digit or a special symbol (other than underscore).
(iii) It cannot contain any special symbol other than underscore.

(iii) Literals

These are the various types of constants that can be used in a program. These include integers, decimal numbers, characters, strings, etc.

Integers- These include all integers on the number line excluding decimals. Eg: 1,0,-2,etc.

Integers can be stored using the following data types: int, long int, short int, byte.

Floating-point numbers-These include all numbers on a real number line. Eg: 1.5, -0.9, etc.

Floating-point numbers are stored in two forms: float, double.

Character Literals-They are single characters enclosed within single quotes. Eg: 'a', '+', '7'.

Character Literals are stored in char type variables.

> **Note: '7' is different from 7. The former is a character while the latter is an integer.**

String Literals-A numbers of characters grouped together form strings. Eg: "abc", "java@123", etc. They are stored in strings.

Boolean Literals-A Boolean literal is either a true or a false value. It is stored in Boolean type of variable.

(iv) Operators

An Operator is used to perform various arithmetical, relational etc. operations on a given set of operands. An expression is defined as an appropriate combination of operators and operands.

Eg:

2	+	3
↓	↓	↓
operand	operator	operand

Arithmetic Operators

These are the operators which are used to perform various mathematical operations. Arithmetical operators include +, -, *, /, %.

Operator	Expression	Result
+	2+3	5
-	6-4	2
*	5*6	30
/	9/3	3
%	7%2	1

> **Note: An integer divided by an integer is always an integer and an integer divided by a real number is always a real number.**

Eg: Consider the following operations:

Operation	Example	Result
Integer/Integer	6/4	1
Integer/Float	6/4.0	1.25
Float/Integer	6.0/4	1.25
Float/Float	6.0/4.0	1.25

Note: The modulus operator prints the remainder.
Eg: 4%2 gives 0 since 4 is completely divisible by 2.

Eg: Consider the following operations:

Operation	Result
4%2	0
2%4	2
-2%4	-2
-2%-4	-2
2%-4	2

When we use the modulus operator, the sign of the result is always the same as the sign of the numerator.

Relational Operators

These are used for making comparisons in between operands. They are of six types:

Operator	Meaning
>	Greater than
<	Less than
>=	Greater than or equal to
<=	Less than or equal to

==	Equal to
!=	Not equal to

Logical Operators

Logical operators are basically used for combining two or more relational operators together for making complex comparisons.

Operator	Meaning
&&	Logical AND
||	Logical OR
!	NOT

Eg: (2<3) && (5<=10), in this expression, we have joined two relational comparisons together by using the logical operator AND.

Increment/Decrement Operators

These are the operators which operate upon only one operand. There are four types of such operators:

(i)   pre-increment
(ii) post-increment
(iii) pre-decrement
(iv) post-decrement

In a prefix expression the operator is placed before the operand and thus the value is first changed then it is used.

Eg:
int x, a=4;
x=++a;

In the above example, the value of a is incremented first and then the new value is stored in x. So, x becomes 5.

While in a postfix expression the operator is placed after the operand and thus the value is first used and then it is changed.

Eg:
int x, a=4;
x=a++;

In the above example, the value of a is first used and then it is incremented. So, x becomes 4.

Assignment Operator

This operator is used the assign the value of an expression to a variable.

Eg:
int x=10;
This will store the value 10 in x.

It is right to left associative. Eg:

int a=b=10;

So first 10 will be stored in b and then the value of b will be stored in a.

(v) Separators

Separators are usually punctuators. Eg:, ;, (), {}, etc.

Eg: int a, b;

In the above statement, is used to separate a and b while ; is used as a terminating statement.

Note: Semicolon (;) is necessary at the end of every statement, otherwise the compiler will report an error.

1.8 EVALUATION OF AN ARITHEMETIC EXPRESSION

Consider an expression like x*2/y+3. Now in this expression ambiguity arises that which operator has to be evaluated first * or / or +. Unfortunately we do not have BODMAS rule which we has in mathematics. In order to resolve this problem, we use the concept of precedence of operators.

1st priority */ %
2nd priority + -

Now consider the expression:

x=10-6/3+8*7-10 //perform /
= 10-2+8*7-10 // perform *
=10-2+56-10 // perform +
=66-2-10 // perform -
= 54

1.9 CONCEPT OF DATA TYPE

Data type, simply as the name says is the type of data. We know that every variable holds some data but the type of data the variable will hold is determined by the data type.

Eg: If '3' is to be stored in 'a' then a should be of integer type, if '3.4' is to be stored in 'a' then a should be of floating type.

There are two types of data types: Primitive and non-primitive.

Primitive data types include integer, character, etc while non-primitive data types include classes and arrays.

Integer Types

Integer types can hold values like 2,3,-45, -563, etc. Depending upon the size of the value we can choose the integer data type.

Type	Size	Min Value	Max Value
byte	1 byte	-128	127

short	2 bytes	-32768	32767
Int	4 byte	-2147483648	2147483647
Long	8 byte	-9223372036854775808	9223372036854775807

Normally we use **int** but it is a good practice to choose the data type depending upon the requirement to save the space.

Floating point types

Floating point types can hold decimal values like 3.14, -6.7, 54.6. Depending upon the precision, they are of two types: float and double.

Type	Size	Min Value	Max Value
Float	4 bytes	3.4e-038	3.4e+0.38
Double	8 bytes	1.7e-308	1.7e+308

Character type

Character type is used store a single character like 'a', 'c'. It is of two bytes and can hold only a single character.

Boolean type

Boolean type can hold only two type of values true or false. It is used when we want to store the true or falsity of a condition. It is of 1 byte.

1.10 COMMENTS

Comments are used in a program wherever you want to add any description to the statement.

Eg:
if we have written

double si=(prin*rate*time)/100;

So we can add a description to it stating that this is the formula to calculation simple interest.

Like,

double si=(prin*rate*time)/100; // formula to calculate interest

Comments are totally ignored by the compiler and they are only used to describe the logic of the program.

In java comments can be given in two ways single line (//) and multi-line. (/* . . . . */)

Try to incorporate this habbit of writing comments in the programs. This will help you to debug your program in case of an error and will help someone else to understand the logic of your program.

1.11 BASIC STRUCTURE OF A PROGRAM

```
public class Program1
{
    public static void main(String args[])
    {
        // set of statements
    }
}
```

The first statement is the **class declaration. class** is a keyword and **Program1** is the name of the class. Since java is an object oriented programming language, everything is written inside a class.

The next thing is the method **main()**. The execution of the program starts from main. A java application may have any number of classes but it will have only one main() method.

main is declared as **static** because it marks the starting point of the program and need not be called by an object.

Inside the main method we can write an executable set of statements as per our requirement.

PROGRAMMING EXAMPLES

Ques. 1.1 Write a program to print 'Java is wonderful'.

```
public class Print
{
    public static void main(String args[])
    {
        System.out.println("Java is wonderful");
    }
}
```

> **Output:** Java is wonderful

Note:

print() method is used to display something on the monitor. There is a misconception that the print() method belongs to the System class but it actually belongs to the **PrintStream class.**

There is a difference between print() and println(). The print() method displays the text on the screen while the println() method displays and then moves the cursor to the next line.

Ques. 1.2 Write a program to add two numbers.

```
public class Add
{
    public static void main(String args[])
    {
        int a=2;
        int b=3;
        int c=a+b;
        System.out.println("The sum is: "+c);
    }
}
```

Output: The sum is: 5

Note:

'int a=2' is used to declare and initialize a variable. It will create a variable named 'a' and the value '2' will be stored in it.

Note the difference between the '+' used in addition and the '+' used in the print statement. The former is an arithmetic operator while the latter is called concatenation operator.

Ques. 1.3 **Write a program to input two numbers from the user and then add them.**

```java
import java.io.*;
public class Add
{
    public static void main(String args[])throws
    IOException
    {
        BufferedReader br=new BufferedReader
        (new InputStreamReader(System.in));
        int a, b;
        System.out.println("Enter the values of a
        and b");
        a=Integer.parseInt(br.readLine());
        b=Integer.parseInt(br.readLine());
        int c=a+b;
        System.out.println("The sum is: "+c);
    }
}
```

> **Input:** a=5, b=8
> **Output:** The sum is: 13

Note:

In Java each and every value that is inputted is in form of a string. So, it has to be converted into integer, float(depending upon our data type) to use it for mathematical operations. The method 'parseInt' converts the value entered by the user to an integer.

Similarly we can also write,
    double a=parseDouble(br.readLine());
The above statement will convert the value into double type.

Practice Question

Ques.1.4 Write a program to input two float numbers and perform basic mathematical operations on them.(i.e Addition, Subtraction, Multiplication and Division)

Ques.1.5 Write a program to print:

```
* * * * * * *
*           *
* * * * * * *
```

Ques.1.6 **Write a program to enter three numbers and find their average.**

```
import java.util.*;
public class Average
  {
      public static void main(String args[])
      {
          canner sc=new Scanner(System.in);
          int a, b, c;
          double avg;
          System.out.println("Enter three numbers");
          a=sc.nextInt();
          b=sc.nextInt();
          c=sc.nextInt();
          avg=(a+b+c)/3;
          System.out.println("The average is: "+avg);
      }
  }
```

> **Input:** a=2,b=3,c=4
> **Output:** The average is :3

Ques.1.7 Write a program to calculate the simple interest (the required parameters should be entered by the user).

> ➤ The simple interest is calculated as:
> S.I.=(Principle*Rate*Time)/100

```java
import java.util.*;
public class Interest
{
    public static void main(String args[])
    {
        Scanner sc=new Scanner(System.in);
        int p, n;
        double r, amt;
        System.out.println("Enter the amount");
        p=sc.nextInt();
        System.out.println("Enter the number of
        years");
        n=sc.nextInt();
        System.out.println("Enter the rate of interest");
        r=sc.nextDouble();
        amt=(p*n*r)/100 ;
        System.out.println("The interest is: "+amt);
    }
}
```

Program Analysis:

You need to have some knowledge regarding what type of a variable is to be used when.

Eg: If we are storing the age of a person then we should use an 'int' type variable rather than a 'double' type. This is because not only it will consume less space but it's also obvious that the age is always a whole number.

In the same way, here we have used 'int' for the number of years and principle amount and 'double' for rate of interest and simple interest.

Input: p=1000,r=8%,t=2
Output: The interst is: 160

Ques 1.8 Write a program to calculate the area of a triangle.

> ➤ The area of the triangle is calculated as:
> Area=$\sqrt{s(s-a)(s-b)(s-c)}$
> where $s=(a+b+c)/2$ and a, b, vc are the sides of the triangle.

```java
import java.io.*;
public class Area
{
    public static void main(String args[])throws
    IOException
    {
        BufferedReader br=new BufferedReader
        (new InputStreamReader(System.in));
        int a, b, c;
        double s, area;
        System.out.println("Enter the value of
        a, b, c");
        a=Integer.parseInt(br.readLine());
        b=Integer.parseInt(br.readLine());
        c=Integer.parseInt(br.readLine());
        s=(a+b+c)/2;
        area=Math.sqrt(s*(s-a)*(s-b)*(s-c));
        System.out.println("The area is: "+area);
    }
}
```

Program Analysis:

In java there are certain pre-defined functions to perform various mathematical operations.

Eg:

int x=Math.pow(2,3);
This will store 2 raised to the power 3 i.e. 8 in x.

int x=Math.sqrt(9);
This will store square root of 9 i.e. 3 in x.

Similarly there are a number of other functions to perform various mathematical operations.

Practice Question

Ques.1.9 Write a program to find the distance between two coordinate points.

> ➤ The required formula is:
> dist=√(x2-x1)*(y2-y1)
> where x1,y1,x2,y2 are the required coordinates.

Ques.1.10 Write a program to calculate the profit percent given the cost price and profit of the article.

Ques 1.11 Write a program to enter the temperature of a city in Fahrenheit and convert it into Centigrade.

> ➤ The required formula is :
> F=(9*C)/5+32

```
import java.util.*;
public class Temperature
{
    public static void main(String args[])
    {
        Scanner sc=new Scanner(System.in);
        double temp1,temp2;
        System.out.println("Enter the temperature in
        fahrenheit");
        temp1=sc.nextInt();
        temp2=((temp1-32)*5)/9;
        System.out.println("The temperature in Celcius : "+temp2);
    }
}
```

Input: temp1=98
Output: The temperature in Celcius is: 36.66

Ques 1.12 **Write a program to enter two numbers and swap their values.**

```java
import java.io.*;
public class Swap
{
    public static void main(String args[])throws IOException
    {
        BufferedReader br=new BufferedReader (new
        InputStreamReader(System.in));
        int a, b, temp;
        System.out.println("Enter two numbers");
        a=Integer.parseInt(br.readLine());
        b=Integer.parseInt(br.readLine());
        System.out.println("The value of a before
        swapping is: "+a);
        System.out.println("The value of b before
        swapping is: "+b);
        temp=a
        a=b;
        b=temp;
        System.out.println("The value of a after swapping
        is: "+a);
        System.out.println("The value of b after swapping
        is: "+b);
    }
}
```

Program Analysis:

Here we have to swap the two numbers by making use of a temporary variable.

Eg: a=10, b=20

Now,

temp=a; // 10
a=b; // 20
b=temp; // 10

Therefore the two numbers are swapped.

> **Input:** a=2,b=3
> **Output:** a=3,b=2

Ques 1.13 Write a program to enter two numbers and swap them without using any third variable.

```java
import java.util.*;
public class Swap
{
    public static void main(String args[])
    {
        Scanner sc=new Scanner(System.in);
        int a, b, temp;
        System.out.println("Enter two numbers");
        a=sc.nextInt();
        b=sc.nextInt();
        System.out.println("The value of a before
        swapping is: "+a);
        System.out.println("The value of b before
        swapping is: "+b);
        a=a+b;
        b=a-b;
        a=a-b;
        System.out.println("The value of a after swapping
        is: "+a);
        System.out.println("The value of b after swapping
        is: "+b);
    }
}
```

Program Analysis:

We have to swap two numbers without making use of any temporary variable.

Eg: a=10, b=20.

Now,

    a=a+b; // 10+20=30
    b=a-b; // 30-20=10
    a=a-b; // 30-10=20

Therefore the two numbers are swapped.

> **Input:** a=2,b=3
> **Output:** a=3,b=2

Ques 1.14 **Write a program to enter the marks in five subjects of a student and then calculate his percentage.**

```java
import java.io.*;
public class Percentage
{
public static void main(String args[])throws IOException
    {
        BufferedReader br=new BufferedReader(new
        InputStreamReader(System.in));
        int m1,m2,m3,m4,m5;
        double per;
        System.out.println("Enter the marks in five
        subjects");
        m1=Integer.parseInt(br.readLine());
        m2=Integer.parseInt(br.readLine());
        m3=Integer.parseInt(br.readLine());
        m4=Integer.parseInt(br.readLine());
        m5=Integer.parseInt(br.readLine());
        per=(m1+m2+m3+m4+m5)/5;
        System.out.println("The percentage is: "+per);
    }
}
```

Input: m1=78,m2=89,m3=67,m4=90
Output: The percentage is: 81

Practice Question

Ques.1.15 Write a program to find the area of a circle.

Ques 1.16 Write a program to enter the basic salary of an employee and then calculate his gross salary(the HRA is 10% of the basic, TA is 8%, DA is 15% of the basic salary).

```java
import java.io.*;
public class Salary
{
public static void main(String args[])throws IOException
    {
        BufferedReader br=new BufferedReader(new
        InputStreamReader(System.in));
        int sal;
        double ta, da, hra, gs;
        System.out.println("Enter the basic salary");
        sal=Integer.parseInt(br.readLine());
        ta=0.08*sal;
        da=0.15*sal;
        hra=0.10*sal;
        gs=sal+ta+da+hra;
        System.out.println("The gross salary : "+gs);
    }
}
```

Note:
   Instead of writing 8/100 we have written 0.08.
   This is because when we divide an integer by an integer the result is always an integer.

Eg:
        double a=3/4;
   Now what do you expect will be stored in 'a', 0.75? No, 0.0 gets stored in 'a'. This is because 3 is an integer and 4 is also an integer so the result is an integer i.e. 0.
   Therefore, 0.0 gets stored in a.
   Because of this reason only we have written 0.08 instead of 8/100.

Ques 1.17 Write a program to generate a random number in java.

```
public class Random
{
    public static void main(String args[])
    {
        double n=Math.random();
        System.out.println(n);
    }
}
```

Practice Question

Ques.1.18 Write a program to print the total bill of the customer.(Enter the no. of units purchased, the price of each unit, discount offered and tax from the user.)

Ques.1.19 Write a program to input a character and print its ASCII value.

```
import java.io.*;
public class ASCII
{
    public static void main(String args[])throws IOException
    {
        BufferedReader br=new BufferedReader(new
        InputStreamReader(System.in));
        char ch;
        System.out.println("Enter a character");
        ch=(char)br.read();
        System.out.println("The ASCII value is:"+(int)ch);
    }
}
```

Program Analysis:

Every character, digit, number, etc. is assigned an ASCII value in java.

Type	ASCII Value
Upper-case alphabets	65-90
Digits	48-57
Lower-case alphabets	97-122

> **Input:** ch='A'
> **Output:** The ASCII value is : 65

Ques.1.20 Write a program to input a character in upper case and print it in lower case.

```
import java.io.*;
public class Case
{
    public static void main(String args[])throws
    IOException
    {
        BufferedReader br=new BufferedReader(new
        InputStreamReader(System.in));
        char ch;
        System.out.println("Enter a character in upper case");
        ch=(char)br.read();
        ch+=32;
        System.out.println("The chracter in lower case is:"+ch);
    }
}
```

Practice Question

Ques.1.21 Write a program to enter the distance in km and convert it into metres, centimetres, milimetres.

1.3 QUESTION HOUR

(i)   What is an object. Give suitable example.
(ii)   What do you mean by abstraction?
(iii) Define Encapsulation.
(iv) What is a Class?
(v)   Why is a class called an object factory?
(vi) Define Byte Code.
(vii) Explain the concept of JVM.
(viii) How is Java platform independent?
(ix) What do you mean by character set?
(x)   What is the difference between operator and operand?
(xi) Explain the various types of operators.
(xii) What is the difference between = and == ?
(xiii) What do you mean by scope of the variable.
(xiv) Explain the various data types with the help of suitable examples.
(xv) Explain bitwise operators.
(xvi) What is the use of Boolean literal.
(xvii) What is a package?

1.4 MULTIPLE CHOICE QUESTIONS

(i) Values/attributes of the characteristics represent _____ of an object.

    (a) State
    (b) Behaviour
    (c) Identity

(ii) The _____ of an object is implemented through functions.

    (a) Characteristic
    (b) Behaviour
    (c) State

(iii) Blue J is an _____.

    (a) IDE(Integrated Development Environment)
    (b) Editor

(c) Compiler

(d) Interpreter

(iv) _____ are the programs embedded in web pages.

(a) Standalone

(b) Applets

(c) HTML

(v) A variable name cannot start with _____.

(a) Alphabet

(b) Digit

(c) Underscore

(vi) Which of the following is an invalid statement:

(a) a=2+3;

(b) a+2=3;

(c) a+=3;

(d) a=b+c;

(vii) a=3/4+2-3*6/3+2 ; The value of a is :

(a) -2

(b) -6

(c) 6

(d) 1

(viii) a=1;
　　　x=++a+a++++a+a ; The value of x is :

(a) 11

(b) 7

(c) 10

(d) 12

(ix) x=2;

   x+=x*x+2-3/4;

  (a) 12

  (b) 23

  (c) None of the above

  (d) 8

(x) What is the output of 8%-3 ?

  (a) 2

  (b) -2

  (c) 0

  (d) Syntax Error

(xi) What is the output of 8/3 ?

  (a) 2.66

  (b) 2

  (c) 2.66666

  (d) Error

(xii) '5' is an:

  (a) character

  (b) string

  (c) integer

  (d) real number

(xiii) What is the size of an int variable ?

  (a) 4 byte

  (b) 8 byte

  (c) 2 byte

  (d) 16 byte

(xiv) Java was developed by :

  (a) Steve Jobs

  (b) Bill Gates

(c) James Gosling
(d) Dennis Richie

(xvi) Existence in more than one form is called:

(a) Encapsulation
(b) Abstraction
(c) Polymorphism
(d) Inheritance

(xvii) The wrapping up of data and functions into a single unit is called:

(a) Encapsulation
(b) Abstraction
(c) Polymorphism
(d) Inheritance

(xviii) Which of the following is a real constant:

(a) 2.3
(b) 'a'
(c) 2
(d) "abc"

(xix) What is the output of 7.5 % 1.5 ?

(a) 0
(b) 1
(c) Syntax Error

(xx) int a='a'+97;

(a) Correct
(b) Wrong

(xxi) int x='c'+'d';

    The value of x is:

(a) 199

(b) cd

(c) Compiler Error

(xxii) float x=789_975;

    True or False ?

(a) True

(b) False

CHAPTER 2

CONDITIONAL PROGRAMMING

- Need of Conditional Programming
- Programming with if-else
- switch-case Construct
- Ternary Operator
- Programming examples
- Short-answer Questions
- Multiple-choice Questions

Programs at a Glance

If & Else

➢ Program to enter a number and check if it is positive, negative or zero.

➢ Program to enter the time from the user and increment it by one second then display the new time.

➢ Program to enter two numbers and print which one of them is greater.

➢ Program to enter three numbers and check which one of them is greater.

➢ Program to input a year and check if it is a leap year or not.

➢ Program to input a character and check if it is an uppercase alphabet, lowercase alphabet, digit or a special character.

➢ Program to input a character and convert it into uppercase if it is in lowercase and vice versa.

➢ Program to enter the age of a candidate and check if he is eligible to vote.

➢ Program to calculate the roots of a quadratic equation.

➢ Program to input three sides of a triangle and check whether a triangle is a valid triangle or not.

➢ Program to enter a date and check if it is a valid date or not.

➢ Program to enter the marks in four subjects and find the grade as per given criteria.

➢ Program to calculate the electricity bill of a house.

➢ Program to calculate to commission of a property broker.

➢ Program to calculate the fine of a student in the library

Switch Case

➢ Program to perform the following operation.(Addition, Subtraction, Multiplication & Division)

➢ Program to input a number and print the corresponding day of the week.

➢ Program to enter a number between 1 and 12 and print the corresponding month.

➢ Program to input an alphabet and check whether it is a vowel or a consonant.

➤ Program to convert the temperature from Centigrade to Fahrenheit or vice versa depending upon user's choice.

Ternary Operator

➤ Program to enter a assign 0 to b if a is less than 10 otherwise assign 1.
➤ Program to enter an alphabet and check if it is lower case alphabet or not.
➤ rogram to find the greatest of three numbers using the ternary operator.

2.1 INTRODUCTION

In real life we encounter many situations when we have to make decisions based on certain conditions. Consider the following example:

A school gives scholarships to those students who get marks above 90 percent in their class. So, only if the condition is fulfilled (or it is true), the scholarship is awarded. Take another example like if you get a good college, your father will give you a bike. It means that getting a bike or not depends upon getting a good college. If you get a good college then you will get a bike otherwise you won't.

Similarly in Java we have conditional statements which execute particular set of code depending upon whether condition is true or false.

In the earlier programs all the statements were executed sequentially. i.e the 1st statement then the 2nd then 3rd and so on. However if we want to alter this sequence, or in other words if we want to decide which statement is to be executed when, we use conditional statements.

The following conditional statements are supported in java:

(i) if statement
(ii) if-else statement
(iii) switch statement
(iv) Ternary Operator

2.2 IF STATEMENT

The if statement is the most basic conditional statement. It is used when we want to execute some statement depending upon the truth or falsity of a condition. The syntax of the if statement is as follows:

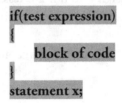

if(test expression)

{

block of code

}

statement x;

In the above syntax, if the test expression evaluates to be true then only, the block of code is executed otherwise it is not.

'statement x' will always be executed whether the condition is true or false. Moreover, one may skip the braces if the block of code is a single line statement.

- **Flowchart**

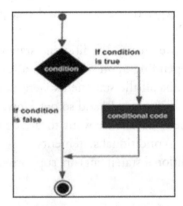

It is quite clear from the figure that the conditional code is executed only when the test expression is true otherwise the part of the code is skipped.

- **Example**

The simple if statement is used in the following piece of code below:

```
if(rank==1)
{
        System.out.println("You earned a
        scholarship! ");
}
```

According to the above code, if the rank of the student is 1, then a scholarship will be awarded to the student.

2.3 IF-ELSE STATEMENT

Sometimes in real life we do a particular task if the condition is fulfilled and an entirely different task if it is not. Eg: If my train ticket gets confirmed i will go by train else, I will go by flight.

The if-else statement is an extension to the simple if statement. With the help of this statement we can execute a particular set of instruction if the test expression is true and a different set of instructions if it is false.

It's syntax is discussed below:

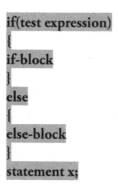

```
if(test expression)
{
if-block
}
else
{
else-block
}
statement x;
```

In the above syntax, if the expression is true then the if-block is executed and if the expression is false, then the else-block is executed. In any case whether the expression is true or false 'statement x' is always executed. And remember, only one block is executed either the 'if' or 'else', in no case both can execute.

- **Flowchart**

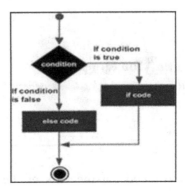

From the above flowchart it is quite clear that the if-block is executed if the condition is true and the else block is executed if the condition is false.

- **Example**

An example further explains the working of if-else statement:

```
if(marks>=40)
        System.out.println("Pass");
else
        System.out.println("Fail");
```

The above block of code prints 'Pass' if the marks are greater than or equal to 40, otherwise it prints 'Fail' i.e. if the marks are less than 40.

2.4 NESTED IF-ELSE

An if-else statement can be nested as per the requirement i.e we can create an if inside and if then again an if inside the if and so on . . .

Eg:

```
if(condition)
{
    if(condition)
        statement;
    else
    statement;
}
```

An if block can also be placed inside the else block.
Eg:

```
if(condition)
    statement;
else
{
    if(condition)
        statement;
    else
        statement;
}
```

They can be nested upto any level depending upon the logic of the program.

2.5 THE ELSE IF LADDER

This is a way of putting ifs together when multipath decisions are involved.
The general form is:

```
if(condition 1)
    //statements
else if(condition 2)
    //statements
```

else if(condition 3)

    //statements

else

    //statements

In this type of construct as soon as a condition is found to be true the statements associated with that block will be executed. If none of the conditions evaluate to be true and the statement of the last **else block** will be executed.

However in no case two blocks can execute.

The major advantage of using this technique is that it is much more readable and understandable and it offers efficiency in terms of time.

Since as soon as a condition becomes true and the block gets executed then, none of the other conditions are checked.

2.6 DANGLING ELSE PROBLEM

Consider the following example,

if(condition 1)

    if(condition 2)

    //statements

    else

    //statements

In the above example, the question arises that the last else is paired with which if? i.e. The statements with the else block will be executed when condition 1 is false or when condition 2 is false.

The else is always paired with the last unpaired if.

In this case if condition 2 is false then the statements associated with the else block will be executed. So, remember to use the braces to avoid any such confusion. This is known as **dangling-else problem**.

PROGRAMMING EXAMPLES

Ques. 2.1 Write a program to enter a number and check if it is positive, negative or zero.

```java
import java.io.*;
public class Number
{
    public static void main(String args[])throws
    IOException
    {
        int num;
        BufferedReader br=new BufferedReader(new
        InputStreamReader(System.in));
        System.out.println("Enter a number");
        num=Integer.parseInt(br.readLine());
        if(num>0)
        System.out.println("The number is positive");
        else if(num<0)
        System.out.println("The number is negative");
        else
        System.out.println("The number is zero");
    }
}
```

> **Input:** num=-1
> **Output:** The number is negative

Ques. 2.2 **Write a program to enter the time from the user and increment it by one second then display the new time.**

> ➤ If the number of seconds are greater than 60, then the minutes should be incremented by 1 accordingly and if the number of minutes are greater than 60 then the number of hours should be incremented consequently.

```java
import java.io.*;
public class TimeIncrement
{
public static void main(String args[])throws IOException
    {
            BufferedReader br=new BufferedReader(new
            InputStreamReader(System.in));
            int hrs, min, sec;
            System.out.println("Enter the hours, minutes
            and seconds");
            hrs=Integer.parseInt(br.readLine());
            min=Integer.parseInt(br.readLine());
            sec=Integer.parseInt(br.readLine());
            sec++;
            if(sec>=60)
            {
                min++;
                sec-=60;
            }
            if(min>=60)
        {
        hrs++;
        min-=60;
        }
            System.out.println("After adding 1 sec, the
```

time is");
System.out.println(+hrs+" hours "+min+"
minutes "+sec+" seconds ");

}

}

> **Input:** hr=5, min=67,sec=80
> **Output:** After incrementing,
> hr=6, min=8,sec=21

Note:
If the time is increased by 1 sec . . . then if the seconds become greater than 60 then 1 has to be incremented in minutes and if the minutes become greater than 60 then 1 has to be added in hours.

Ques. 2.3 Write a program to enter two numbers and print which one of them is greater.

```
import java.io.*;
public class Greater
{
public static void main(String args[])throws IOException
    {
        int a, b;
        BufferedReader br=new BufferedReader(new
        InputStreamReader(System.in));
        System.out.println("Enter two numbers");
        a=Integer.parseInt(br.readLine());
        b=Integer.parseInt(br.readLine());
        // test condition
        if(a>b)
        System.out.println(a+" is greater than "+b);
        else if(a<b)
        System.out.println(b+" is greater than "+a);
        else
        System.out.println("Both are equal");
    }
}
```

Input: a=2,b=7
Output: b is greater

Ques. 2.4 **Write a program to enter three numbers and check which one of them is greater.**

```java
import java.util.*;
public class Greatest
{
public static void main(String args[])
    {
        int a, b, c;
        Scanner sc=new Scanner(System.in);
        System.out.println("Enter three numbers");
        a=sc.nextInt();
        b=sc.nextInt();
        = sc.nextInt();
        // two conditions joined using logical operators
        if((a>b) && (a>c))
        System.out.println(a+" is greatest");
        else if((b>a) && (b>c))
        System.out.println(b+" is greatest");
        else
        System.out.println(c+" is greatest");
    }
}
```

> **Input:** a=9,b=3,c=4
> **Output:** a is greater

Note:
The above program can also be done in this way:
```java
        max=a;
        if(b>max)
                max=b;
        if(c>max)
                max=c;
        System.out.println(max+" is greatest");
```

Ques. 2.5 Write a program to input a year and check if it is a leap year or not.

```
import java.io.*;
public class Year
{
public static void main(String args[])throws IOException
    {
        int yy;
        BufferedReader br=new BufferedReader(new
        InputStreamReader(System.in));
        System.out.println("Enter a year");
        yy=Integer.parseInt(br.readLine());
        // check if the year is divisible by 4
        if(yy%4==0)
        System.out.println("It is a leap year");
        else
        System.out.println("It is not a leap year");
    }
}
```

Note:
The complete condition to test whether the year is a leap year or not can be written as:

```
        if(yy%4==0 && (yy%100==0||yy%400==0))
            System.out.println("It is a leap year");
        else
            System.out.println("It is not a leap
            year");
```

Input: yy=2000
Output: It is a leap year

Ques. 2.6 Write a program to input a character and check if it is an uppercase alphabet, lowercase alphabet, digit or a special character.

```java
import java.io.*;
public class Character
{
public static void main(String args[])throws IOException
    {
        char
        ch;
        BufferedReader br=new BufferedReader(new
        InputStreamReader(System.in));
        System.out.println("Enter a character");
        ch=(char)br.read();
        if(ch>='A' && ch<='Z')
                System.out.println("It is an upper case
                alphabet");
        else if(ch>='a' && ch<='z')
                System.out.println("It is a lower case
                alphabet");
        else if(ch>='0' && ch<='9')
                System.out.println("It is a digit");
        else
                System.out.println("It is a special
                character");
    }
}
```

Input: ch=a
Output: It is a lower case character

Practice Question

Ques.2.7 Write a program to input a character and convert it into uppercase if it is in lowercase and vice versa.

Ques.2.8 Write a program to enter the age of a candidate and check if he is eligible to vote.

```
import java.util.*;
public class Vote
  {
      public static void main(String args[])
        {
            int age;
            Scanner sc=new Scanner(System.in):
            System.out.println("Enter the age");
            age=sc.nextInt();
            if(age>=18)
            // a candidate is eligible to vote if theage is above 18
                System.out.println("Eligible");
            else
                System.out.prinltn("Not Eligible");
        }
  }
```

Input: age=11
Output: Not eligible

Ques. 2.9 Write a program to calculate the roots of a quadratic equation.

```java
import java.util.*;
public class Quadratic
{
public static void main(String args[])
    {
        int a, b, c;
        double d, r1, r2;
// r1 and r2 are the roots of the equation
        Scanner sc=new Scanner(System.in);
        System.out.println("Enter the values of a, b and c");
        a=sc.nextInt();
        b=sc.nextInt();
        c= sc.nextInt();
        d=(b*b)-(4*a*c);
// It is the discriminant of the quadratic equation
        if(d==0)
        {
            r1=r2=-b/(2*a);
            System.out.println("The roots are equal:
            "+r1+" "+r2);
        }
        else if(d>0)
        {
            r1=(-b+Math.sqrt(d))/(2*a);
            r2=(-b-Math.sqrt(d))/(2*a);
            System.out.println("The roots are real
            and distinct: "+r1+" "+r2);
        }
        else
            System.out.println("The roots are imaginary");
    }
}
```

Ques. 2.10 Write a program to input three sides of a triangle and check whether a triangle is a valid triangle or not.

> ➤ A triangle is said to be valid if sum of the two sides of the triangle is always greater than the third side.

```java
import java.io.*;
public class Triangle
{
public static void main(String args[])throws IOException
    {
        int a, b, c;
    // a, b, c are the lengths of the sides of the triangle
        BufferedReader br=new BufferedReader(new
        InputStreamReader(System.in));
        System.out.println("Enter the length of the
        sides of triangle");
        a=Integer.parseInt(br.readLine());
        b=Integer.parseInt(br.readLine());
        c=Integer.parseInt(br.readLine());
        if((a+b)>c || (b+c)>a || (a+c)>b)
            System.out.println("It is a valid triangle");
        else
            System.out.println("It is not a valid triangle");
    }
}
```

Input: a=2,b=3,c=4
Output: It is a valid triangle

Ques.2.11 Write a program to enter a date and check if it is a valid date or not.

```java
import java.io.*;
public class DateValidate
{
public static void main(String args[])throws IOException
    {
        BufferedReader br=new BufferedReader(new
        InputStreamReader(System.in));
        int d, m, y;
        boolean flag=false;
        System.out.println("Enter the day, month and year");
        d=Integer.parseInt(br.readLine());
        m=Integer.parseInt(br.readLine());
        y=Integer.parseInt(br.readLine());
        if((m==1||m==3||m==5||m==7||m==8||m==
        10||m==12) && (d>=1 && d<=31))
                flag=true;
        else if((m==4||m==6||m==9||m==11) &&
        (d>=1 && d<=31))
                flag=true;
        else if( m==2 &&(y%4==0)&&(d>=1 && d<=29))
                flag=true;
        else if((m==2 && y%4!=0) && (d>=1 &&
        d<=28))
                flag=true;
        if(flag==true)
                System.out.println("It is a valid date");
        else
                System.out.println("It is not a valid date");
    }
}
```

Ques. 2.12 **Write a program to enter the marks in four subjects and find the grade as follows:**

Percentage	Grade
>=90	A
>=75 and <90	B
>=50 and <75	C
<50	D

```java
import java.io.*;
public class Grade
{
public static void main(String args[])throws IOException
    {
        int m1,m2,m3,m4;
        BufferedReader br=new BufferedReader(new
        InputStreamReader(System.in));
        System.out.println("Enter the marks in four subjects");
        m1=Integer.parseInt(br.readLine());
        m2=Integer.parseInt(br.readLine());
        m3=Integer.parseInt(br.readLine());
        m4=Integer.parseInt(br.readLine());
// the following statement will calculate the student's percentage
        double per=(m1+m2+m3+m4)/4.0;
        if(per>=90)
                System.out.println("Grade A");
        else if(per>=75 && per<90)
                System.out.println("Grade B");
        else if(per>=50 && per<75)
                System.out.println("Grade C");
        else
                System.out.println("Grade D");
    }
}
```

> **Input:** m1=89, m2=90, m3=78, m4=86
> **Output:** Grade B

Ques. 2.13 Write a program to calculate the electricity bill of a house as follows:

UNITS	RATE
First 100 units	0.50 per unit
Next 100 units	0.60 per unit
Above 200 units	0.80 per unit

```java
import java.util.*;
public class Bill
{
public static void main(String args[])
    {
        double units, amt;
        Scanner sc=new Scanner(System.in);
        System.out.println("Enter the number of units consumed");
        units=sc.nextInt();
        if(units<=100)
            amt=units*0.50;
        else if(units>100 && units<=200)
            amt=(100*0.50)+((units-100)*0.60);
        else
            amt=(100*0.50)+(100*0.60)+((units-200)*0.80);
            amt=amt+300;
        System.out.println("The total amount is "+amt);
    }
}
```

Ques. 2.14 Write a program to calculate to commission of a property broker.

DEAL	COMMISSION
<=500000	5%
>500000 and <=1000000	6.5%
>1000000 and <=2000000	8.0%
>2000000	10%

```java
import java.io.*;
public class Commission
{
public static void main(String args[])throws IOException
    {
        int amt;
        double comm;
        BufferedReader br=new BufferedReader(new
        InputStreamReader(System.in));
        System.out.println("Enter the amount of deal");
        amt=Integer.parseInt(br.readLine());
        if(amt<=500000)
            comm=0.05*amt;
        else if(amt>500000 && amt<=1000000)
            comm=0.065*amt;
        else if(amt>1000000 && amt<=2000000)
            comm=0.08*amt;
        else
            comm=0.10*amt;
        System.out.println("The commission is "+comm);
    }
}
```

> **Input:** amt=650000
> **Output:** The commission is : 42250

Ques. 2.15 Write a program to calculate the fine of a student in the library as follows:

DELAY	FINE
First 10 days	Rs.2 per day
Next 5 days	Rs.3 per day
Later than 15 days	Rs.5 per day

```java
import java.util.*;
public class Library
 {
 public static void main(String args[])
     {
         int days, fine;
         Scanner sc=new Scanner(System.in);
         System.out.println("Enter the number of days
         the book is returned late");
         days=sc.nextInt();
         if(days<=10)
                 fine=2*days;
         else if(days>10 && days<=15)
                 fine=(2*10)+(3*(days-10));
         else
                 fine=(2*10)+(3*5)+(5*(days-15));
         System.out.println("The fine is "+fine);
     }
 }
```

Input: days=12
Output: The fine is: Rs.26

2.7 SWITCH STATEMENT

The if Statement is easy to use when the number of conditions we need to check for a certain problem are less, but as the number of conditions we need to check increases and the alternates available also increase, our program tends to become more complex and for such programs we have the option of using the switch statement. The switch statement can be used to test the value of a particular expression against a list of particular case values.

The syntax is as follows:

```
switch(expression)
{
        case 1st_value:
        block 1;
        break;
        case 2nd_value:
        block 2;
        break;
        default:
        default block;
        break;
}
```

In the above syntax, the various different values of the "expression" we expect are represented by 1st_value,2nd_value and so on. Depending upon these values, a particular block of code is executed. It is generally used when we want to compare a value against a list of case values. Moreover, switch gives us the capability of a default block which is executed when none of the other cases are met.

Another important point in the syntax is the use of break, if this is neglected, once a case is met, all cases below it will also be executed even if they are not met. This is called as **fall-through.**

Eg:

```
switch(expression)
{
    case 1: //statements
    case 2: //statements
        break;
    default: //statements
}
```

In the above example if the expression matches with the value of the first case then, not only the statements with the first case are executed but also with the second case. This is because of the absence of the break statement after case 1.

- **Flowchart**

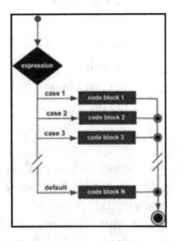

- **Example**

A simple block of code employing switch statement is given below:

```
switch(n)
{
        case 1:
        System.out.println("Hi !");
        break;
        case 2:
        System.out.println("Hello");
        break;
        case 3:

    System.out.println("How are you ?");
    break;
    default:
    System.out.println("Invalid Choice");
}
```

In the above piece of code an appropriate message will be printed depending upon the value of x i.e. if the value of x is 2 then the message 'Hello' will be displayed on the screen.

PROGRAMMING EXAMPLES

Ques. 2.16 Input two numbers from the user. Write a menu driven program to perform the following operation.

1-Addition
2-Subtraction
3-Multiplication
4-Division

```
import java.io.*;
public class Calculator
 {
public static void main(String args[])
throws IOException
    {
        int ch, a, b;
        double c;
        BufferedReader br=new BufferedReader
        (new InputStreamReader(System.in));
        System.out.println("Enter two numbers");
        a=Integer.parseInt(br.readLine());
        b=Integer.parseInt(br.readLine());
        System.out.println("Press 1 for addition");
        System.out.println("Press 2 for subtraction");
        System.out.println("Press 3 for multipication");
        System.out.println("Press 4 for division");
        System.out.println("Enter your choice");
        ch=Integer.parseInt(br.readLine());
        switch(ch)
        {
            case 1:
            c=a+b;
            System.out.println("The sum is "+c);
```

```
break;
case 2:
c=a-b;
System.out.println("The difference is "+c);
break;
case 3:
c=a*b;
System.out.println("The product is "+c);
break;
case 4:
c=a/b;
System.out.println("The quotient is "+c);
break;
default:
System.out.println("Invalid Entry");
}
}
}
```

Ques. 2.17 Write a program to input a number and print the corresponding day of the week.

```java
import java.util.*;
public class Week


{
public static void main(String args[])
    {
        int num;
        Scanner sc=new Scanner(System.in);
        System.out.println("Enter a number");
        num=sc.nextInt();
        switch(num)
        {
            case 1:
            System.out.println("Monday");
            break;
            case 2:
            System.out.println("Tuesday");
            break;
            case 3:
            System.out.println("Wednesday");
            break;
            case 4:
            System.out.println("Thursday");
            break;
            case 5:
            System.out.println("Friday");
            break;
            case 6:
            System.out.println("Saturday");
            break;
```

```
case 7:
System.out.println("Sunday");
break;
default:
System.out.println("Invalid Entry");
        }
    }
}
```

Practice Question

Ques.2.18 Write a program to enter a number between 1 and 12 and print the corresponding month.

Ques. 2.19 **Write a program to input an alphabet and check whether it is a vowel or a consonant.**

```java
import java.io.*;
public class Vowel
{
public static void main(String args[])
throws IOException
    {
        char ch;
        BufferedReader br=new BufferedReader
        (new InputStreamReader(System.in));
        System.out.println("Enter an alphabet");
        ch=(char)br.read();
        switch(ch)
        {
            case 'a':
            case 'e':
            case 'i':
            case 'o':
            case 'u':
                    System.out.println("It is a vowel");
            break;
            default:
                    System.out.println("It is a consonant");
        }
    }
}
```

Input: ch=e
Output: It is a vowel

Ques. 2.20 Write a program to convert the temperature from Centigrade to Fahrenheit or vice versa depending upon user's choice.

```
import java.io.*;
public class Temperature
{
public static void main(String args[])
throws IOException
    {
        int ch;
        BufferedReader br=new BufferedReader
        (new InputStreamReader(System.in));
        System.out.println("Press 1 to convert from
        fahrenheit to celcius");
        System.out.println("Press 2 to convert from
        celcius to fahrenheit");
        System.out.println("Enter your choice");
        ch=Integer.parseInt(br.readLine());
        double temp1,temp2;
        switch(ch)
        {
            case 1:
            System.out.println("Enter the
            temperature in Fahrenheit");
            temp1=Double.parseDouble(br.readLine());
            temp2=((temp1-32)*5)/9;
            System.out.println("The temperature in
            Celcius is "+temp2);
            break;
            case 2:
            System.out.println("Enter the temperature in
            Celcius");
            temp1=Double.parseDouble(br.readLine());
```

```
temp2=((9*temp1)/5)+32;
System.out.println("The temperature in
Fahrenheit is "+temp2);
break;
default:
System.out.println("Invalid Entry");
}
}
}
```

2.8 TERNARY OPERATOR

Commonly called the conditional operator, is represented by **? :** and is used to make decisions which on evaluation of the test expression have one of only two results, or two-way decisions. The syntax for the ternary operator is given below:

test_expression ? expression_1 : expression_2

In the syntax, firstly, the test expression is evaluated and if found to be true, expression_1 is evaluated otherwise expression_2 is evaluated.

- **Example:**

---

marks>40 ? System.out.println("Pass"): System.out.println("Fail");

Therefore, if marks are greater than 40,then "Pass" is printed otherwise "Fail" is printed.

PROGRAMMING EXAMPLES

Ques.2.21 Write a program to enter a assign 0 to b if a is less than 10 otherwise assign 1.

```
import java.util.*;
public class Assign
{
public static void main(String args[])
    {
        int a;
        Scanner sc=new Scanner(System.in);
        System.out.println("Enter a number");
        a=Integer.parseInt(br.readLine());
        int b;
        b=a<10?0:1;
        System.out.println("The value of b is "+b);
    }
}
```

Input: a=12   **Output:** b=1

Ques.2.22 **Write a program to enter an alphabet and check if it is lower case alphabet or not.**

```java
import java.io.*;
public class CharacterTernary
{
public static void main(String args[])throws IOException
    {
        char ch;
        int flag;
        BufferedReader br=new BufferedReader(new
        InputStreamReader(System.in));
        System.out.println("Enter a character");
        ch=(char)br.read();
        flag=ch>='a'?(ch<='z'?1:0):0;
        if(flag==1)
                System.out.println("It is a lower case alphabet");
        else
                System.out.println("It is not a lower case alphabet");
    }
}
```

```
Input: ch=h
Output: It is a lower case alphabet
```

Practice Question

Ques.2.23 Write a program to find the greatest of three numbers using the ternary operator.

Ques.2.24 Write a program to enter a number and check if it is even or odd.

2.6 QUESTION HOUR

(i)   What is the use of if statement?
(ii)   What is the difference between if and switch?
(iii)   Why is ternary operator normally not used?
(iv)   Explain the dangling else problem?
(v)   What is the use of default case in switch?
(vi)   What is the major drawback of switch statement?
(vii)   Explain fall-through.
(viii) Explain the nesting of if statement.
(ix)   Explain the drawback of ternary operator.
(xi)   Is fall through an advantage or disadvantage?
(xii)   Give a program that shows the use of fall through.
(xiii) Which has better efficiency, if or switch?

2.7 MULTIPLE CHOICE QUSETIONS

Ques. Choose the correct option:

(i) int x=0;
     if(x>0)
         System.out.println("Hi");
         System.out.println("Hello");

   (a) Hi
   (b) Hello
   (c) Hi
       Hello

(ii) int a=1;
     if(a>1)
         System.out.println("Hi");
else
         System.out.println("Hello");

   (a) Hi
   (b) Hello
   (c) Hi

Hello
(d) No output

(iii) int n=1; if(n==1)
  System.out.println("Computer");
   System.out.println("Applications");
   else
   System.out.println("Java");

(a) Computer
(b) Computer Applications
(c) Java
(d) Syntax Error

(iv) int n=1;
 if(n==1)
   System.out.println("Computer");
 else
   System.out.println("Applications");
 System.out.println("Java");

(a) Computer Java
(b) Applications Java
(c) Syntax Error

(v) if(true)
   System.out.println("Hello");
 else
   System.out.println("World");

(a) Hello
(b) World
(c) Compiler Error

(vi) int a=2,b=3;
 if(a==2 || b<0)
   System.out.println("Java is wonderful");
 else
   System.out.println("Java is great");

(a) Java is wonderful
(b) Java is great
(c) Java is wonderful
   Java is great

(vii) int a=2,b=3;
```
    if(a==2 && b<0)
        System.out.println("Java is wonderful");
    else
        System.out.println("Java is great");
```

(a) Java is wonderful
(b) Java is great
(c) Java is wonderful
   Java is great

(viii) if(!true)
```
        System.out.println("Hello");
    else
        System.out.println("World");
```

(a) Hello
(b) World
(c) Compiler Error

(ix) int m=1,n=5;
```
    if(m==1 && n>10)
        System.out.println("Java");
    else if(m>=1 || n>10)
        System.out.println("Master");
    else
        System.out.println("Client");
```

(a) Java
(b) Master
(c) Client
(d) None of the above

(x) int a=2,b=a;
    if(a>b)
        System.out.println("Great");
    else if(a<b)
        System.out.println("Less");
    else
        System.out.println("Equal");

(a) Great
(b) Less
(c) Compiler Error
(d) Equal

(xi) double d=3.0;
    if(d<1);
        System.out.println("Programming");

(a) Programming
(b) Syntax Error
(c) No output

(xii) double d=3.0;
    if(d<1);
        System.out.println("Programming");
    else
        System.out.println("Concepts");

(a) Programming
(b) Syntax Error
(c) No output
(d) Concepts

(xiii) if(97<'z')
        System.out.println("ASCII");
    else
        System.out.println("Unicode");

(a) ASCII
(b) Unicode

(c) Syntax Error

(xiv)
```java
char ch='c';
switch(ch)
{
case 'a':
    System.out.println("Vowel");
    break;
case 'b':
    System.out.println("Consonant");
    break;
case 'c':
    System.out.println("Consonant");
    break;
}
```

(a) Vowel

(b) Consonant

(c) No output

(xv)
```java
int z=3;
switch(z)
{
case 1:
    System.out.println("One");
    break;
case 2:
    System.out.println("Two");
case 3:
    System.out.println("Three");
}
```

(a) One

(b) Two

(c) Two
    Three

(d) Three

(xvi) int n=0;
    m=(n==0?1:0)
    System.out.println(m);

(a) 1
(b) 0
(c) Syntax Error

CHAPTER 3

ITERATIVE PROGRAMMING

- Introduction to loops
- for loop
- while loop
- do-while loop
- use of break and continue
- programs involving iteration
- Multiple-choice questions

Programs At a Glance

➢ Program to print 'Java is wonderful' 5 times.
➢ Program to find x^n, where x and n are entered by the user.
➢ Program to find the sum of first 10 natural numbers.
➢ Program to find the sum of first 50 even numbers.
➢ Program to print the table of a given number.
➢ Program to find the sum of numbers between m and n, where m and n are entered by the user.
➢ Program to find the sum of squares of the numbers from 1 to n, where the value of n is entered by the user.
➢ Program to display all the leap years from 1800 to 1900.
➢ Program to find the divisors of a number.
➢ Program to generate Fibonacci series upto n terms.
➢ Program to keep on entering the numbers from the user till the user enters a negative number.
➢ Program to find the sum of all positive and negative numbers entered by the user.
➢ Program to find the HCF of two numbers entered by the user.
➢ Program to enter two numbers and find their LCM.
➢ Program to calculate the electricity bill of the customers as per entered by the user.

3.1 INTRODUCTION

In our daily life we do a number of things repeatedly. Eg: Brushing your teeth, going to school, watching television, etc. We repeat a number of things in our day to day life depending upon our requirements.

In the programming world also, at certain situation there is a need to repeat a particular number of statements a given number of times. This means a statement will repeat a particular number of times depending upon a condition. When the condition is true, the statements are executed and when the condition is false, the loop is not executed.

A loop is used if we want to repeat a particular instruction a number of times depending upon certain conditions. In looping a sequence of statements are executed until some conditions for the termination of the loop are satisfied. Therefore, a loop consists of two segments, one known as the body of the loop and the other known as control statement.

Depending upon the position of the control statement, loops are of two types:
- (i) Entry-controlled Loops
- (ii) Exit-controlled Loops

3.2 ENTRY CONTROLLED LOOP

In an entry-controlled loop, the condition is tested before the execution of the body of the loop. If the condition is not satisfied then the body of the loop will not be executed, otherwise the body of the loop will continue to get executed till the condition is true.

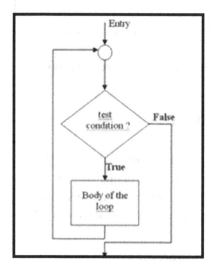

They are of two types:
- (i) For Loop
- (ii) While Loop

3.3 EXIT CONTROLLED LOOP

In an exit-controlled loop, the body of the loop is executed till the condition is true. But the condition is tested at the end of the therefore the body of the loop is executed unconditionally for the first time. In this type of loop, one time execution of the body is guaranteed.

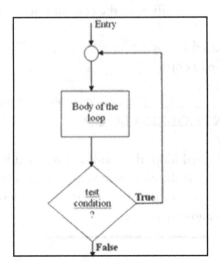

Do-while is an example of an exit-controlled loop.

3.4 FOR STATEMENT

The for loop is an entry-controlled loop. The body of the for loop is executed till the test condition remains true. It is generally used when the number of iterations are known to us i.e. we know how many times the loop has to execute. The basic syntax of the for loop is as follows:

for(initialization ; test expression; increment)
    {
        body of the loop
    }

The body of the loop will be executed until the condition is false.

In the for loop, initialization, test expression, increment all are optional i.e. any of them can be omitted but still the loop will work the same.

Eg: if we have to print "Hello" five times then it can be done in the following ways:

(i) for(int i=1;i<=5;i++) // nothing omitted
     System.out.println("Hello");

(ii) int i=1;
      for(; i<=5;i++) // initialization omitted
        System.out.println("Hello");

(iii) int i=1;
      for(; ; i++) // initialization, test expression omitted
      {
        if(i>5)
        break;
        System.out.println("Hello");
      }

(iv) int i=1;
     for(; ;) // all omitted
     {
        if(i>5)
        break;
        System.out.println("Hello");
        i++;
     }

(v) for(; ;)
     {
        //empty body
     }
This is an example of infinite loop discussed later in this chapter.

3.5 WHILE STATEMENT

It is an entry-controlled loop. It is used when the number of iterations are unknown i.e. we don't know how many times the body is to be executed.

The syntax is as follows:

```
while(test expression)
{
    body of the loop
}
```

The body of the loop will be executed till the condition is true.

3.6 DO-WHILE STATEMENT

It is an exit-controlled loop. It is used when the number of iterations are unknown.

The syntax is as follows:

```
do
    {
        body of the loop
    } while( test expression );
```

Since the condition is tested at the end of the loop, the body of the loop will always be executed atleast once. Note that the semicolon is necessary after the test expression.

3.7 COMPARISON BETWEEN ALL THREE LOOPS

Although the working of all the loops is same but they vary in their syntax. Let us see it with the help of an example.

Eg: Program to print the numbers from 1 to 5.

Using for

```
for(int i=1;i<=5;i++)
    System.out.println(i);
```

Using while

```java
int i=1;
while(i<=5)
{
    System.out.println(i);
    i++;
{
```

Using do-while

```java
int i=1;
do
{
    System.out.println(i);
    i++;
}while(i<=5);
```

3.8 THE BREAK STATEMENT

A break statement is used to jump out of a loop while the test expression is still true. It is generally used in situations where we want to terminate the loop without checking the test condition.

```java
for(int i=1;i<=5;i++)
{
    //statement 1
    // statement 2
    break;
    //statement 3;
}
```

In the above loop, statement 3 will not be executed, because the break statement will terminate the loop and the control will not reach this statement.

Eg:

```
for(int i=0;i<10;i++)
{
    System.out.print(i);
    if(i>5)
        break;
}
```

The above code will print 1 2 3 4 5 6 only. This is because when i becomes 6, the if condition is true and the loop gets terminated.

Therefore the break statement is used to jump out of the body of the loop before the loop has completed its full cycle.

3.9 THE CONTINUE STATEMENT

The continue statement forces the next iteration of the loop ignoring the statements which are still left to be executed.

Eg:

```
for(int i=0;i<10;i++)
{
    if(i<5)
        continue;
    System.out.print(i);
}
```

The above code will print 5 6 7 8 9. This is because till the time the value of i is less than 5 the control is transferred to the beginning of the loop ignoring the print statement.

```
for(int i=1;i<=5;i++)
{
    //statement 1
    // statement 2
    continue;
    //statement 3;
}
```

In the above program, the continue statement will force the next iteration of the loop because of which the statement 3 will not be executed.

3.10 INFINITE LOOPS

Sometimes, in certain situations we want non-terminating loop i.e. an infinite loop. Such loops may also be used to generate time delays.

An infinite loop can be created in many ways like:

```
for( ; ; )
{
    //body
}
```

OR

```
while(true)
{
    //body
}
```

However in case we want to terminate from an infinite loop then it can be done easily with the help of the break statement.

3.11 NESTED LOOPS

Just like if-else, loops can also be nested inside one another. We can have a for loop inside a for loop, a for loop inside while, a while inside do-while, etc.

Eg:

```
for( // parameters)
{
    // statements
    for( // parameters)
        //statements
```

```
    //statements
}
```

OR

```
while( // test expression)
{
    //statements
    for(// parameters)
        //statements
    //statements
}
```

In this way loops can be nested depending upon the logic of the program.

PROGRAMMING EXAMPLES

Ques.3.1 Write a program to print 'Java is wonderful' 5 times.

```
public class Print
 {
public static void main(String args[])
    {
        for(int i=1;i<=5;i++)
        {
            System.out.println("Java is wonderful");
        }
    }
}
```

Program Analysis:

```
        ┌──────  for(int i=1;i<=5;i++) ──────┐  true
        │          {                          │
        │                    System.out.println("Java is wonderful");
        │          }
        └────►
```
false

Till the time the condition is true, the body of the loop will execute and when the condition becomes false the loop will terminate.

Ques.3.2 Write a program to find x^n, where x and n are entered by the user.

```java
import java.io.*;
public class Power
{
public static void main(String args[])throws IOException
    {
        int x, n, y=1;
        BufferedReader br=new BufferedReader(new
        InputStreamReader(System.in));
        System.out.println("Enter the value of x and n");
        x=Integer.parseInt(br.readLine());
        n=Integer.parseInt(br.readLine());
        for(int i=1;i<=n;i++)
        {
            y=y*x;
        }
        System.out.println(x+" ^ "+n+" = "+y);
    }
}
```

Input: x=3,n=2
Output: 9

Ques.3.3 Write a program to find the sum of first 10 natural numbers.

```java
import java.io.*;
public class Sum
 {
 public static void main(String args[])throws IOException
    {
        int s=0;
        for(int i=1;i<=10;i++)
        {
            s=s+i;
        }
        System.out.println("The sum is "+s);
    }
}
```

Program Analysis:

$$\underline{1 + 2} = 3 \qquad \underline{3+4}=7 \qquad \underline{7+5}=12$$

$$\downarrow \qquad\qquad \downarrow \qquad\qquad \downarrow$$

1st iteration   2nd iteration   3rd iteration

. . . and so on

Practice Question

Ques.3.4 Write a program to find the sum of first 50 even numbers.

Ques.3.5 Write a program to print the table of a given number.

```java
import java.util.*;
public class Table
{
public static void main(String args[])
    {
        int n, p;
        Scanner sc=new Scanner(System.in);
        System.out.println("Enter a number");
        n=sc.nextInt();
        for(int i=1;i<=10;i++)
        {
            p=n*i;
            System.out.println(n+" * "+i+" = "+p);
        }
    }
}
```

Ques.3.6 Write a program to find the sum of numbers between m and n, where m and n are entered by the user.

```java
import java.io.*;
public class SumNumbers
{
public static void main(String args[])
throws IOException
    {
        int m, n, sum=0;
        BufferedReader br=new BufferedReader
        (new InputStreamReader(System.in));
        m=Integer.parseInt(br.readLine());
        n=Integer.parseInt(br.readLine());
        for(int i=m;i<=n;i++)
        {
            sum+=i;
        }
        System.out.println("The sum is "+sum);
    }
}
```

Program Analysis:

Eg: m=2, n=5

1st iteration:
```java
for(i=2;i<=5;i++)
{
    sum=0+2; // 2
}
```

2nd iteration: Now i becomes 3,
for(; 3<=5;i++)
{

    sum=2+3; // 5

}

3rd iteration: Now i becomes 4,
for(; 4<=5;i++)
{

    sum=5+4; // 9

}

4th iteration: Now i becomes 5,
for(; 5<=5;i++)
{

    sum=9+5; // 14

}

Input: m=10, n=15
Output: The sum is:75

Ques.3.7 **Write a program to find the sum of squares of the numbers from 1 to n, where the value of n is entered by the user.**

```java
import java.util.*;
public class SumSquares
 {
 public static void main(String args[])
    {
        Scanner sc=new Scanner(System.in);
        int s=0,n;
        System.out.println("Enter a the value of n");
        n=sc.nextInt();
        for(int i=1;i<=n;i++)
         s=s+(i*i);
        System.out.println("The sum of squares is "+s);
    }
 }
```

> **Input:** 5
> **Output:** The sum is: 55

Practice Question

Ques.3.8 Write a program to display all the leap years from 1800 to 1900.

Ques.3.9 **Write a program to find the divisors of a number.**

```java
import java.util.*;
public class Divisors
 {
 public static void main(String args[])
    {
        int n;
        Scanner sc=new Scanner(System.in);
        System.out.println("Enter a number");
        n=sc.nextInt();
        System.out.println("The divisors are");
        for(int i=1;i<=n;i++)
        {
            if(n%i==0)
            System.out.println(i);
        }
    }
}
```

Program Analysis:

Eg: n=4;

4%1==0	4%2==0	4%3!=0
↓	↓	↓
1st iteration	2nd iteration	3rd iteration
(Divisor Found)	(Divisor Found)	(Divisor not Found)

Ques.3.10 Write a program to generate Fibonacci series upto n terms.

```java
import java.io.*;
public class Series
{
public static void main(String args[])throws IOException
    {
        int n;
        BufferedReader br=new BufferedReader(new
        InputStreamReader(System.in));
        System.out.println("Enter the value of n");
        n=Integer.parseInt(br.readLine());
        int a=0,b=1,c;
        System.out.print(a);
        System.out.print(b);
        for(int i=1;i<=n-2;i++)
        {
            c=a+b;
            a=b;
            b=c;
        System.out.print(c);
        }
    }
}
```

| Input:n=7 |
| Output: 0112358 |

Ques.3.11 Write a program to keep on entering the numbers from the user till the user enters a negative number.

```java
import java.io.*;
public class Number
{
public static void main(String args[])
throws IOException
    {
        int n;
        BufferedReader br=new BufferedReader
        (new InputStreamReader(System.in));
        do
        {
            System.out.println("Enter a number");
            n=Integer.parseInt(br.readLine());
            if(n<0)
            {
                System.out.println("Program Terminated");
                break;
            }
            else
                System.out.println("The number you
                entered is "+n);
        }while(true);
    }
}
```

Program Analysis:

do
{

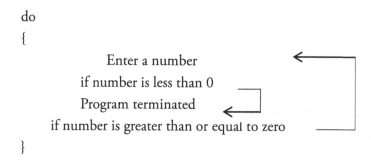

           Enter a number

       if number is less than 0

       Program terminated

   if number is greater than or equal to zero

}

Ques.3.12 Write a program to find the sum of all positive and negative numbers entered by the user. (The program is terminated if the user enters 0)

```java
import java.io.*;
public class Average
{
public static void main(String args[])
throws IOException
    {
        int n, sum_pos=0,sum_neg=0;
        BufferedReader br=new BufferedReader
        (new InputStreamReader(System.in));
        do
        {
            System.out.println("Enter a number");
            n=Integer.parseInt(br.readLine());
            if(n==0)
            {
                System.out.println("Program Terminated");
                break;
            }
            else if(n>0)
                sum_pos+=n;
            else
                sum_neg+=n;
        }while(true);
        System.out.println("The sum of positive
        numbers is "+sum_pos);
        System.out.println("The sum of negative numbers is "+sum_neg);
    }
}
```

Ques.3.13 Write a program to find the HCF of two numbers entered by the user.

```
import java.io.*;
public class HCF
{
public static void main(String args[])
throws IOException
    {
        BufferedReader br=new BufferedReader
        (new InputStreamReader(System.in));
        int a, b, c, hcf=0;
        System.out.println("Enter the first number");
        a=Integer.parseInt(br.readLine());
        System.out.println("Enter the second number");
        b=Integer.parseInt(br.readLine());
        c=a>b ?a:b;
        for(int i=1;i<=c;i++)
        {
            if (a%i==0 && b%i==0 && i>hcf)
            hcf=i;
        }
        System.out.println("The H.C.F. is: "+hcf);
    }
}
```

```
Input: a=10,b=6
Output: The HCF is: 2
```

Ques.3.14 Write a program to enter two numbers and find their LCM.

```java
import java.io.*;
public class LCM
{
public static void main(String args[])
throws IOException
    {
        BufferedReader br=new BufferedReader
        (new InputStreamReader(System.in));
        int a, b, c, lcm;
        System.out.println("Enter the first number");
        a=Integer.parseInt(br.readLine());
        System.out.println("Enter the second number");
        b=Integer.parseInt(br.readLine());
        c=a*b;
        lcm=c;
        for(int i=1;i<=c;i++)
        {
            if (i%a==0 && i%b==0 && i<lcm)
            lcm=i;
        }
        System.out.println("The L.C.M. is: "+lcm);
    }
}
```

> **Input:** a=10,b=6
> **Output:** The LCM is:30

Ques.3.15 Write a program to calculate the electricity bill of the customers as per entered by the user.

```java
import java.io.*;
public class Bill
{
public static void main(String args[])
throws IOException
    {
        double units, amt;
        int n;
        BufferedReader br=new BufferedReader
        (new InputStreamReader(System.in));
        System.out.println("Enter the number of customers");
        n=Integer.parseInt(br.readLine());
        for(int i=1;i<=n;i++)
        {
            System.out.println("Enter the number of
            units consumed for customer no."+i);
            units=Integer.parseInt(br.readLine());
            if(units<=100)
                amt=units*0.50;
            else if(units>100 && units<=200)
                amt=(100*0.50)+((units-100)*0.60);
            else
                amt=(100*0.50)+(100*0.60)+((units-200)*0.80);
                amt=amt+300;

            System.out.println("The total amount for
            customer no."+i+" is "+amt);
        }
    }
}
```

Ques.3.16 **Write a program to print the equivalent characters of the ASCII values from 0 to 255.**

```java
import java.io.*;
public class Print
{
    public static void main(String args[])throws
    IOException
    {
        for(int i=0;i<=255;i++)
        {
            System.out.println("ASCII equivalent char of "+i+" is
            "+(char)i);

        }
    }
}
```

Practice Question

Ques.3.17 Write a program to input 10 numbers and print the range. (Range is the difference between the largest and the smallest number.)

3.9 QUESTION HOUR

(i) What is the use of looping statements?
(ii) Explain all three types of looping statements along with their syntax.
(iii) What is the difference between entry and exit controlled loops?
(iv) What is the difference between while and do-while?
(v) What is the difference between for and while?
(vi) Explain the use of counter variable.
(vii) Illustrate the use of infinite loop with the help of an example.
(viii) Explain the concept of nested loops.

3.10 MULTIPLE CHOICE QUESTIONS

Ques. Choose the correct option:

(i) Repeating a particular statement a particular number of times is called _____.

(a) Looping
(b) Conditional Programming
(c) Inheritance
(d) Abstraction

(ii) When we know the number of iterations we use _____ loop.

(a) while
(b) do-while

(iii) for(int i=1;i<=5;i++)
     System.out.print(i);

(a) 12345
(b) 12344
(c) 11111
(d) None of the above

(iv) for(int i=1;i<10;)
```
    {
        System.out.print(i);
        i+=2;
    }
```

(a) 11111
(b) 12345
(c) 13579
(d) 246810

(v) int i=2;
```
    for( ; i<10 ; )
    {
        System.out.print(i);
        i+=2;
    }
```

(a) 2222
(b) 2468
(c) 12345
(d) Syntax Error

(vi) for(; ;)
```
    {
    }
```

(a) Infinite Loop
(b) Syntax Error
(c) No output

(i) int s=0;
```
    for(int i=1;i<4;i++)
    {
        for(int j=1;j<=i;j++)
        {
            s=s+j;
        }
    }
```

```
System.out.println(s);
```

(a) 8
(b) 7
(c) 5
(d) 10

(vii)
```
int i=1;
while(i<5)
{
    System.out.print(i);
    i+=2;
}
```

(a) 13
(b) 135
(c) 1234
(d) 12345

(viii)
```
int n=0;
while(true)
{
    System.out.println("Hi!");
    break;    }
```

(a) Hi!
(b) Infinite loop
(c) Syntax Error

(ix)
```
int i=1;
while(true)
{
    if(i<5)
    System.out.print(i);
    else
    break;
}
```

(a) 1 2 3 4 5
(b) 1 2 3 4 5 6 7 8 9 ...
(c) 1 2 3 4

(x) int i=1;
     while(i<10)
     {
         if(i<5)
         continue;
         System.out.print(i);
     }

(a) 1 2 3 4 5 6 7 8 9
(b) 1 2 3 4 5
(c) 5 6 7 8 9

CHAPTER 4

NUMBER-BASED PROGRAMMING

Programs At a Glance

- ➤ Program to enter a number and check if it is even or odd.
- ➤ Program to enter a number and check if it is positive, negative or zero.
- ➤ Program to enter a number and find its factorial.
- ➤ Program to enter a number and check if it is prime or not.
- ➤ Program to print all the twin prime numbers between 1 and 100.
- ➤ Program to enter a number and print its reverse.
- ➤ Program to enter a number and find the sum of its digits.
- ➤ Program to enter a number and check if it's palindrome or not.
- ➤ Program to print all the palindrome numbers between 1 and 1000.
- ➤ Program to enter a number and check if it's an Armstrong number or not.
- ➤ Program to enter a binary number and convert it to decimal.
- ➤ Program to enter a decimal number and convert it to binary.
- ➤ Program to enter a decimal number and find its hexadecimal equivalent.
- ➤ Program to enter a hexadecimal number and convert it into its equivalent decimal.
- ➤ Program to enter a number and make it a palindrome.
- ➤ Program to enter a number and check if it's a perfect number or not.
- ➤ Program to enter five positive numbers and print which one of them is greatest.
- ➤ Program to enter a number in decimal and convert it into octal.
- ➤ Program to enter a program in octal and convert it into decimal.
- ➤ Program to find the sum of all even digits of a number.
- ➤ Program to enter a number and check whether it is an evil number or not.
- ➤ Program to enter a number and find the factorial of its digits.
- ➤ Program to enter a number and check if a number is abundant or deficient.
- ➤ Program to input a number and increment each of its digits by 1.
- ➤ Program to input a number and print only the even digits.
- ➤ Program to enter a number and check if it is a special number or not.

4.1 INTRODUCTION

Ever thought how many types of numbers are there. Well don't try counting them, they are enormous in number. Let's try to know about some of them and design their respective programs.

PROGRAMMING EXAMPLES

Ques.4.1 **Write a program to enter a number and check if it is even or odd.**

> ➤ A number is said to be even if it is divisible by 2 and odd if it is not divisible by two.
>
> Eg: 6 is an even number since it is divisible by 2.

```
import java.io.*;
public class EvenOdd
{
    public static void main(String args[])throws
    IOException
    {
        int num;
        BufferedReader br=new BufferedReader(new
        InputStreamReader(System.in));
        System.out.println("Enter a number");
        num=Integer.parseInt(br.readLine());
        if(num%2==0)
        System.out.println("It is an even number");
    else
        System.out.println("It is an odd number");
    }
}
```

Program Analysis:

Examine the following statement,

num%2==0.

We know that the modulus(%) operator returns the remainder. So when we have to check whether a particular number(say a) is divisible by another number(say b) then we computer a%b.

If a%b is equal to zero then, the number is divisible otherwise it's not.

> **Input:** num=11
> **Output:** It is an odd number

Practice Question

Ques.4.2 Write a program to enter a number and check if it is positive, negative or zero.

Ques.4.3 **Write a program to enter a number and find its factorial.**

> The factorial of a number is calculated as:

Factorial of 5 = 5 * 4 * 3 * 2 * 1 = 120

```java
import java.io.*;
public class Factorial
{
    public static void main(String args[])throws
    IOException
    {
        int num, f=1;
        BufferedReader br=new BufferedReader(new
        InputStreamReader(System.in));
        System.out.println("Enter a number");
        num=Integer.parseInt(br.readLine());
        for(int i=1;i<=num;i++)
            f=f*i;
        System.out.println("The factorial is "+f);
    }
}
```

Program Analysis:

Eg: if n=4

1 * 1 =1	1*2=2	2*3=6	3*4=24
↓	↓	↓	↓
1st iteration	2nd iteration	3rd iteration	4th iteration

Input: num=5
Output: The Factorial is: 120

Ques.4.4 Write a program to enter a number and check if it is prime or not.

> A number is said to be prime if it is divisible only by 1 and itself.

Eg: 5 is a prime number since it is divisible only by 1 and 5.

```java
import java.util.*;
public class Prime
{
    public static void main(String args[])
    {
        Scanner sc=new Scanner(System.in);
        int n, c=0;
        System.out.println("Enter a number");
        n=sc.nextInt();
            for(int i=1;i<=n;i++)
            {
                if(n%i==0)
                c++;
            }
            if(c==2)
                System.out.println("It is a prime number");
            else
                System.out.println("It is not a prime number");
    }
}
```

Program Analysis:

The variable 'c' is used to store the total factors of the number. Every time n%i is equal to 0 i.e. a factor is found, the value of c is incremented by 1.

Now if c is equal to 2 i.e. the number has only two factors then it's a prime number otherwise it is not.

Input: n=7
Output: It is a prime number.

Practice Question

Ques.4.5 Write a program to print all the twin prime numbers between 1 and 100.

Ques.4.6 **Write a program to enter a number and print its reverse.**

```java
import java.io.*;
public class Reverse
{
    public static void main(String args[])throws
    IOException
    {
        int num, r ,s=0;
        BufferedReader br=new BufferedReader(new
        InputStreamReader(System.in));
        System.out.println("Enter a number");
        num=Integer.parseInt(br.readLine());
        while(num>0)
        {
            r=num%10;
            s=(s*10)+r;
            num=num/10;
        }
        System.out.println("The reverse is "+s);
    }
}
```

Program Analysis:

The main logic of the program is inside the while loop.

Since we don't know the number of iterations so we use while loop instead of for.

Eg: Suppose num=123.

Now let us the see the working of the loop.

1st iteration:
while(123>0) //true

```
{
    r=123%10; // 3
    s=(0*10)+3; // 3
    num=123/10; //12
}
```

2nd iteration:
```
while(12>0)
{
    r=12%10; //2
    s=(3*10)+2; //32
    num=12/10; //1
}
```

3rd iteration:
```
while(1>0)
{
    r=1%10; //1
    s=(32*10)+1; //321
    num=1/10; //0
}
```
Now the loop terminates. So 's' i.e. 321 is the required reverse of the number.

Input: num=123
Output: The reverse is 321

Ques.4.7 Write a program to enter a number and find the sum of its digits.

```
import java.io.*;
public class Sum
{
    public static void main(String args[])throws
    IOException
    {
        int num, r, s=0;
        BufferedReader br=new BufferedReader(new
        InputStreamReader(System.in));
        System.out.println("Enter a number");
        num=Integer.parseInt(br.readLine());
        while(num>0)
        {
            r=num%10;
            s=s+r;
            num=num/10;
        }
        System.out.println("The sum of digits is "+s);
    }
}
```

> **Input:** num=123
> **Output:** The sum of digits is: 6

Ques.4.8 **Write a program to enter a number and check if it's palindrome or not.**

> ➢ A palindrome is a number which is the same if read in reverse.
>
> Eg: 121, 111, etc.

```
import java.io.*;
public class Palindrome
{
    public static void main(String args[])throws
    IOException
    {
        int num, r, s=0,n;
        BufferedReader br=new BufferedReader(new
        InputStreamReader(System.in));
        System.out.println("Enter a number");
        num=Integer.parseInt(br.readLine());
        n=num;
        while(num>0)
        {
            r=num%10;
            s=(s*10)+r;
            num=num/10;
        }
        if(n==s)
            System.out.println("It is a Palindrome");
        else

            System.out.println("It is not a Palindrome");
    }
}
```

Program Analysis:

The above program was designed for number palindromes. However, we also have string palindromes like "mom", "nitin", etc. The program for string palindrome has been discussed in chapter 9.

Input: num=777
Output: It is a Palindrome

Practice Question

Ques.4.9 Write a program to print all the palindrome numbers between 1 and 1000.

Ques.4.10 Write a program to enter a number and check if it is an Armstrong number or not.

> ➤ An Armstrong is a number whose sum of cubes of the digits is equal to the number.
>
> Eg: 153.

```java
import java.io.*;
public class Armstrong
{
    public static void main(String args[])throws
    IOException
    {
        int num, r, s=0,n;
        BufferedReader br=new BufferedReader(new
        InputStreamReader(System.in));
        System.out.println("Enter a number");
        num=Integer.parseInt(br.readLine());
        n=num;
        while(num>0)
        {
            r=num%10;
            s=s+(r*r*r);
            num=num/10;
        }
        if(n==s)
            System.out.println("It is an Armstrong Number");
        else
            System.out.println("It is not an Armstrong Number");
    }
}
```

Program Analysis:

Let us the see the working of the loop.

1ˢᵗ iteration:
```
while(153>0) //true
{
    r=153%10; // 3
    s=0+(3*3*3); //27
    num=153/10; //15
}
```

2ⁿᵈ iteration:
```
while(15>0)
{
    r=15%10; //5
    s=27+(5*5*5); //152
    num=15/10; //1
}
```

3ʳᵈ iteration:
```
while(1>0)
{
    r=1%10; //1
    s=152+(1*1*1); //153
    num=1/10; //0
}
```
Now the loop terminates. So 's' i.e. 153 is the required Armstrong number.

> **Input:** num=153
> **Output:** It is an Armstrong number

Ques.4.11 Write a program to enter a binary number and convert it to decimal.

```java
import java.io.*;
public class BinarytoDecimal
{
    public static void main(String args[])throws
    IOException
    {
        int num, r, i=0;
        double s=0;
        BufferedReader br=new BufferedReader(new
        InputStreamReader(System.in));
        System.out.println("Enter a number");
        num=Integer.parseInt(br.readLine());
        while(num>0)
        {
            r=num%10;
            s=s+r*Math.pow(2,i);
            num=num/10;
            i++;
        }
        System.out.println("The decimal representation is: "+(int)s);
    }
}
```

Program Analysis:

Consider the following binary number (1001). Now to convert it into decimal perform the following operation.

Firstly add indexes to each digit of the number like,

1	0	0	1
3	2	1	0

Now multiply each digit with 2 raised to the power index and then add them all i.e.

1	0	0	1
$1*(2^3)$	$0*(2^2)$	$0*(2^1)$	$1*(2^0)$

Now add them all,
8+0+0+1=9, which is the required decimal number.

> **Input:** num=101
> **Output:** The decimal representation is 5

Ques.4.12 Write a program to enter a decimal number and convert it to binary.

```java
import java.io.*;
public class Decimaltobinary
{
        public static void main(String args[])throws
        IOException
        {
                int num, r;
                String s="";
                BufferedReader br=new BufferedReader(new
                InputStreamReader(System.in));
                System.out.println("Enter a number");
                num=Integer.parseInt(br.readLine());
                while(num>0)
                {
                        r=num%2;
                        s=r+s;
                        num=num/2;
                }
                System.out.println("The binary representation is:"+s);
        }
}
```

Program Analysis:

Consider the following decimal number(9). Now to convert it into binary, perform the following operation.

Now, continuously keep on dividing the number by 2 and collect the remainders.

Eg:

```
2 | 9
2 | 4   1    ↑
2 | 2   0    |
2 | 1   0    |
2 | 0   1    |
```

Now write the remainders in reverse order. This is the required binary number.

> **Input:** num=5
> **Output:** The binary representation is 101

Practice Question

Ques.4.13 Write a program to enter a decimal number and find its hexadecimal equivalent.

Ques.4.14 Write a program to enter a hexadecimal number and convert it into its equivalent decimal.

Ques.4.15 Write a program to enter a number and make it a palindrome.

```java
import java.io.*;
public class MakePalin
{
        public static void main(String args[])throws
        IOException
        {
                int num, r, s=0,n;
                BufferedReader br=new BufferedReader(new
                InputStreamReader(System.in));
                System.out.println("Enter a number");
                num=Integer.parseInt(br.readLine());
                while(true)
                {
                        n=num;
                        while(num>0)
                        {
                                r=num%10;
                                s=(s*10)+r;
                                num=num/10;
                        }
                        if(n==s)
                        {
                                System.out.println(s+" is a new made
                                Palindrome");
                                break;
                        }
                        else
                        {
                                num=n+s;
                                s=0;
                        }
                }
        }
}
```

Program Analysis:

In order to make a number palindrome, keep on adding the reverse of the number to the number till it becomes a palindrome.
Eg: num=512

We know that 512 is not a palindrome.
Now num=num+reverse of num i.e.
num=512+215=727(palindrome)

Therefore to make a number palindrome, recursively add the number to its reverse till it becomes a palindrome.

Ques.4.16 Write a program to enter a number and check if it's a perfect number or not.

> A number is said to be perfect if the sum of the factors of the number(excluding that number) is equal to the number.

```java
import java.io.*;
public class Perfect
{
        public static void main(String args[])throws
        IOException
        {
                int num, s=0;
                BufferedReader br=new BufferedReader(new
                InputStreamReader(System.in));
                System.out.println("Enter a number");
                num=Integer.parseInt(br.readLine());
                for(int i=1;i<num;i++)
                {
                        if(num%i==0)
                                s=s+i;
                }
                if(num==s)
                        System.out.println("It is a Perfect number");
                else
                        System.out.println("It is not a Perfect number");
        }
}
```

Input: num=6
Output: It is a perfect number

Ques.4.17 Write a program to enter five positive numbers and print which one of them is greatest.

```java
import java.io.*;
public class Greatest
{
        public static void main(String args[])throws
        IOException
        {
            int num, max=0;
            BufferedReader br=new BufferedReader(new
            InputStreamReader(System.in));
            System.out.println("Enter five numbers");
            for(int i=1;i<=5;i++)
            {
                    num=Integer.parseInt(br.readLine());
                    if(num>max)
                        max=num;
            }
            System.out.println("The maximum number is: "+max);
        }
}
```

Practice Question

Ques 4.18 Write a program to enter a number in decimal and convert it into octal.

Ques.4.19 Write a program to enter a program in octal and convert it into decimal.

Ques.4.20 Write a program to find the sum of all even digits of a number.

```java
import java.io.*;
public class SumEven
{
        public static void main(String args[])throws
        IOException
        {
                int num, r, s=0;
                BufferedReader br=new BufferedReader(new
                InputStreamReader(System.in));
                System.out.println("Enter a number");
                num=Integer.parseInt(br.readLine());
                while(num>0)
                {
                        r=num%10;
                        if(r%2==0)
                                s=s+r;
                        num=num/10;
                }
                System.out.println("The sum of even digits is "+s);
        }
}
```

> **Input:** num=24567
> **Output:** The sum of even digits is: 12

Ques.4.21 Write a program to enter a number and check whether it is an evil number or not.

> ➤ A number is said to be evil if after converting the number into binary, the number of 1's in it are even.

```
import java.io.*;
public class Evil
{
        public static void main(String args[])throws
        IOException
        {
                int num, r, c=0;
                BufferedReader br=new BufferedReader(new
                InputStreamReader(System.in));
                System.out.println("Enter a number");
                num=Integer.parseInt(br.readLine());
                while(num>0)
                {
                        r=num%2;
                        if(r==1)
                                c++;
                        num=num/2;
                }
                if(c%2==0)
                        System.out.println("It is an Evil number");
                else
                        System.out.println("It is not a an Evil number");
        }
}
```

Program Analysis:

In order to check whether a number is evil or not, firstly convert the number into binary and then count the number of 1's in it. If they are even it means it is an evil number otherwise its not.

Eg: num=5

Now,

1ˢᵗ iteration:
while(5>0)
{
      r=5%2; // 1
      if(1==1)
         c++; // 1
      num=5/2; //2
}

2ⁿᵈ iteration:

while(2>0)
{
      r=2%2; //0
      if(0==1) // false
      c++;
      num=2/2; //1
}

3ʳᵈ iteration:
while(1>0)
{
      r=1%2; // 1
      if(1==1)
      c++; //2
      num=1/2; // 0
}

Now, if c is divisible by two i.e. the number has even number of 1's then it is an evil number.

Input: num=5 **Output:** It is an evil number.

Practice Question

Ques.4.22 Write a program to enter a number and find the factorial of its digits.

Ques.4.23 Write a program to enter a number and check if a number is abundant or deficient.

```java
import java.io.*;
public class Abundant
{
        public static void main(String args[])throws
        IOException
        {
            int num;
            BufferedReader br=new BufferedReader(new
            InputStreamReader(System.in));
            System.out.println("Enter a number");
            num=Integer.parseInt(br.readLine());
            int s=0;
            for(int i=1;i<num;i++)
            {
                    if(num%i==0)
                    s=s+i;
            }
            if(s>num)
                    System.out.println("It is an abundant number");
            else
                    System.out.println("It is a deficient number");
        }
}
```

Ques.4.24 Write a program to input a number and increment each of its digits by 1.

```java
import java.io.*;
public class Increment
{
        public static void main(String args[])throws
        IOException
        {
                int num;
                BufferedReader br=new BufferedReader(new
                InputStreamReader(System.in));
                System.out.println("Enter a number");
                num=Integer.parseInt(br.readLine());
                String s="";
                int r;
                while(num>0)
                {
                        r=num%10;
                        s=(r+1)+s;
                        num=num/10;
                }
                System.out.println("After incrementing, the number is "+s);
        }
}
```

> **Input:** num=254
> **Output:** After incrementing the number is : 365

Practice Question

Ques.4.25 Write a program to input a number and print only the even digits.

Ques. 4.26 Write a program to enter a number a check if it is a special number or not.

> A number is said to be special if the sum of the factorial of the digits is equal to the number.
> Eg: 145= 1!+4!+5!.

```java
import java.io.*;
public class Special
{
        public static void main(String args[])throws
        IOException
        {
                int num, fact=1,sum=0,r;
                BufferedReader br=new BufferedReader(new
                InputStreamReader(System.in));
                System.out.println("Enter a number");
                num=Integer.parseInt(br.readLine());
                int n=num;
                while(num>0)
                {
                        fact=1;
                        r=num%10;
                        for(int i=1;i<=r;i++)
                                fact=fact*i;
                        sum+=fact;
                        num=num/10;
                }
                if(n==sum)
                        System.out.println("It is a special number");
                else
                        System.out.println("It is not a special number");
        }
}
```

Input: num=145
Output: It is a special number

CHAPTER 5

SERIES SOLUTION

Programs at a Glance

➢ **Program to solve the following series:**

- $1+2+3+ \ldots +n$.
- $1+x+x^2+ \ldots x^n$.
- $1+2^2+3^3+ \ldots x^n$
- $1+1/2+1/3+ \ldots 1/n$
- $1/1! + ½! +1/3! + \ldots 1/n!$
- $1+3+8+ \ldots +n$ (n is the number of terms)
- $x+x^2/2!+x^3/3!+ \ldots x^{n/n!}$
- $2-4+6-8+ \ldots n$ terms
- $1-x^2/2!+x^4/4!+ \ldots n$ terms
- $1+2/2^n+3/3^n+ \ldots n$ terms
- $1+(1+2)+(1+2+3)+ \ldots +(1+2+3+4+ \ldots +n)$
- $1+(1+4)+(1+4+9)+ \ldots (1+4+9+ \ldots +n^2)$
- $(1+2)/(1*2) +(1+2+3)/(1*2*3)+ \ldots (1+2+3+4+ \ldots +n)/(1*2*3*4* \ldots *n)$
- $x!/2+(x+2)!/4+(x+4)!/6+ \ldots (x+n)!/n+2$
- $3+8+15+24+ \ldots n$ terms
- (xvi) $1+\sqrt{x}+\sqrt{x^2}+ \ldots \sqrt{x^{n-1}}$
- (xvii) $1,8,27,64 \ldots n$. (n is the number of terms)
- (xviii) $x+2/x+x/3+4/x \ldots n$ terms.

PROGRAMMING EXAMPLES

Ques.5.1 Write a Java program to solve the following series:

(i) $1+2+3+ \ldots +n$.

```
import java.io.*;
public class Series1
{
        public static void main(String args[])throws
        IOException
        {
                int n, sum=0;
                BufferedReader br=new BufferedReader(new
```

```
            InputStreamReader(System.in));
            System.out.println("Enter the value of n");
            n=Integer.parseInt(br.readLine());
            for(int i=1;i<=n;i++)
            {
                    sum=sum+i;
            }
            System.out.println("The sum is: "+sum);
        }
}
```

Program Analysis:

The variable sum will calculate the final sum of the series and n will be the number of terms in the series.

The loop will work as follows:

1st iteration:
```
for( i=1; i<=4;i++)
{
      sum=sum+i; // 0+1=1
}
```

2nd iteration:
```
for( i=2; i<=4;i++)
{
      sum=sum+i; // 1+2=3
}
```

3rd iteration:
```
for( i=3; i<=4;i++)
{
      sum=sum+i; // 3+3=6
}
```

4th iteration:
```
for( i=1; i<=4;i++)
```

```
{
        sum=sum+i; // 6+4=10
}
```

Input: n=4
Output: The sum is: 10

(ii) $1+x+x^2+ \ldots x^n$.

```
import java.io.*;
public class Series2
{
        public static void main(String args[])throws
        IOException
        {
                int x, n;
                double sum=0;
                BufferedReader br=new BufferedReader(new
                InputStreamReader(System.in));
                System.out.println("Enter the value of x and n");
                x=Integer.parseInt(br.readLine());
                n=Integer.parseInt(br.readLine());
                for(int i=0;i<=n;i++)
                {
                        sum=sum+Math.pow(x ,i);
                }
                System.out.println("The sum is: "+sum);
        }
}
```

Input: x=2, n=3
Output: The sum is: 7

(iii) $1+2^2+3^3+ \ldots x^n$

```
import java.io.*;
public class Series3
```

```
{
        public static void main(String args[])throws
        IOException
        {
                int n;
                double sum=0;
                BufferedReader br=new BufferedReader(new
                InputStreamReader(System.in));
                System.out.println("Enter the value of n");
                n=Integer.parseInt(br.readLine());
                for(int i=1;i<=n;i++)
                {
                        sum=sum+Math.pow(i, i);
                }
                System.out.println("The sum is: "+sum);
        }
}
```

> **Input:** n=4
> **Output:** The sum is: 288

(iv) 1+1/2+1/3+ ... 1/n

```
import java.io.*;
public class Series4
{
        public static void main(String args[])throws
        IOException
        {
                int n;
                BufferedReader br=new BufferedReader(new
                InputStreamReader(System.in));
                System.out.println("Enter the value of n");
                n=Integer.parseInt(br.readLine());
                double sum=0;
                for(double i=1;i<=n;i++)
                {
                        sum=sum+1/i;
```

```
    }
    System.out.println("The sum is "+sum);
  }
}
```

Note: i is declared as double type because if 'i' is an integer then, 1/i i.e. ½, ¼ will yield 0. (Since integer by integer is integer)

Input: n=3
Output: The sum is: 1.83

Practice Question

(v) $1/1! + 1/2! + 1/3! + \ldots 1/n!$

(vi) 1+3+8+ . . . +n (n is the number of terms)

(vii) $x+x^2/2!+x^3/3!+ \ldots x^n/n!$

```java
import java.io.*;
public class Series7
{
        public static void main(String args[])throws
        IOException
        {
                int n, fact;
                double x;
                BufferedReader br=new BufferedReader(new
                InputStreamReader(System.in));
                System.out.println("Enter the value of x and n");
                x=Double.parseDouble(br.readLine());
                n=Integer.parseInt(br.readLine());
                double sum=0;
                for(int i=1;i<=n;i++)
                {
                        fact=1;
                        for(int j=1;j<=i;j++)
                                fact=fact*j;
                        sum=sum+(Math.pow(x, i)/fact);
                }
                System.out.println("The sum is "+sum);
        }
}
```

Program Analysis:

Suppose n=3, x=2.
1st iteration:
```java
for( i=1; i<=3;i++)
{
        fact=1;
        for(int j=1;j<=1;j++)
                fact=fact*j;
        //fact =1
        sum=sum+(Math.pow(2,1)/1); // 2
}
```

2nd iteration:

```
for( i=2; i<=3;i++)
{
        fact=1;
        for(int j=1;j<=2;j++)
                fact=fact*j;
        //fact =2
        sum=sum+(Math.pow(2,2)/2); // 2+2=4
}
```

3rd iteration:

```
for( i=3; i<=3;i++)
{
        fact=1;
        for(int j=1;j<=3;j++)
                fact=fact*j;
        //fact =6
        sum=sum+(Math.pow(2,3)/6); // 4+1.33=5.33
}
```

> **Input:** x=2,n=3
> **Output:** The sum is: 5.33

(viii) 2-4+6-8+ . . . n terms

```
import java.io.*;
public class Series6
{
        public static void main(String args[])throws
        IOException
        {
                int n, s=2;
                double sum=0;
                BufferedReader br=new BufferedReader(new
                InputStreamReader(System.in));
                System.out.println("Enter the value of n");
                n=Integer.parseInt(br.readLine());
                for(int i=1;i<=n;i++)
```

```
        {
                if(i%2==0)
                        sum=sum-s;
                else
                        sum=sum+s;
                s=s+2;
        }
        System.out.println("The sum is: "+sum);
    }
}
```

> **Input:** n=4
> **Output:** The sum is: -4

(ix) 1-x²/2!+x⁴/4!+ . . . n terms

```
import java.io.*;
public class Series9
{
        public static void main(String args[])throws
        IOException
        {
                int n, x, fact=1,s=2;
                double sum=1,c;
                BufferedReader br=new BufferedReader(new
                InputStreamReader(System.in));
                System.out.println("Enter the value of x");
                x=Integer.parseInt(br.readLine());
                System.out.println("Enter the value of n");
                n=Integer.parseInt(br.readLine());
                for(int i=1;i<=n;i++)
                {
                        for(int j=1;j<=s;s++)
                                fact=fact*j;
                        c=Math.pow(x, s)/fact;
                        if(i%2==0)
                                sum=sum-c;
                        else
```

```
            sum=sum+c;
       s=s+2;
   }
   System.out.println("The sum is: "+sum);
  }
}
```

> **Input:** x=3,n=3
> **Output:** The sum is: 3.375

(x) $1+2/2^n+3/3^n+\ldots$ n terms

```
import java.io.*;
public class Series10
{
    public static void main(String args[])throws
    IOException
    {
        int n;
        double sum=0,c;
        BufferedReader br=new BufferedReader(new
        InputStreamReader(System.in));
        System.out.println("Enter the value of n");
        n=Integer.parseInt(br.readLine());
        for(int i=1;i<=n;i++)
        {
            c=Math.pow(i, n);
            sum=sum+(i/c);
        }
        System.out.println("The sum is: "+sum);
    }
}
```

> **Input:** n=3
> **Output:** The sum is: 1.36

(xi) 1+(1+2)+(1+2+3)+ . . . +(1+2+3+4+ . . . +n)

```java
import java.io.*;
public class Series11
{
        public static void main(String args[])throws
        IOException
        {
                int n, c, sum=0;
                BufferedReader br=new BufferedReader(new
                InputStreamReader(System.in));
                System.out.println("Enter the value of n");
                n=Integer.parseInt(br.readLine());
                for(int i=1;i<=n;i++)
                {
                        c=0;
                        for(int j=1;j<=i;j++)
                        {
                                c=c+j;
                        }
                        sum=sum+c;
                }
                System.out.println("The sum is: "+sum);
        }
}
```

Input: n=3
Output: The sum is: 10

Practice Question

(xii) $1+(1+4)+(1+4+9)+\ldots(1+4+9+\ldots+n^2)$

(xiii) $(1+2)/(1*2) + (1+2+3)/(1*2*3) +$
$\ldots (1+2+3+4+ \ldots +n)/(1*2*3*4* \ldots *n)$

```java
import java.io.*;
public class Series13
{
        public static void main(String args[])throws
        IOException
        {
                int n, s1, s2;
                double sum=0;
                BufferedReader br=new BufferedReader(new
                InputStreamReader(System.in));
                System.out.println("Enter the value of n");
                n=Integer.parseInt(br.readLine());
                for(int i=1;i<=n;i++)
                {
                        s1=0;
                        s2=1;
                        for(int j=1;j<=i;j++)
                        {
                                s1=s1+j;
                                s2=s2*j;
                        }
                        sum=sum+(s1/s2);
                }
                System.out.println("The sum is: "+sum);
        }
}
```

> **Input:** n=2
> **Output:** The sum is: 2.5

(xiv) $x!/2+(x+2)!/4+(x+4)!/6+ \ldots (x+n)!/n+2$

```java
import java.io.*;
public class Series14
{
        public static void main(String args[])throws
```

IOException
{

```
int n, s=2, x, fact=1;
double sum=0;
BufferedReader br=new BufferedReader(new
InputStreamReader(System.in));
System.out.println("Enter the value of x");
x=Integer.parseInt(br.readLine());
System.out.println("Enter the value of n");
n=Integer.parseInt(br.readLine());
for(int i=1;i<=n;i++)
{
        for(int j=1;j<=x;j++)
                fact=fact*j;
        x+=2;
        sum=sum+(fact/s);
        s+=2;
}
System.out.println("The sum is: "+sum);
```

}
}

> **Input:** x=1,n=3
> **Output:** The sum is: 22

(xv) 3+8+15+24+ . . . n terms

```
import java.io.*;
public class Series15
{
        public static void main(String args[])throws
        IOException
        {
                int n, c=2;
                double sum=0;
                BufferedReader br=new BufferedReader(new
                InputStreamReader(System.in));
                System.out.println("Enter the value of n");
                n=Integer.parseInt(br.readLine());
```

```
for(int i=1;i<=n;i++)
{
        sum=sum+(c*c)-1;
        c++;
}
System.out.println("The sum is: "+sum);
    }
}
```

Input: n=3
Output: The sum is: 26

Practice Question

(xvi) $1+\sqrt{x}+\sqrt{x^2}+ \ldots \sqrt{x^{n-1}}$

(xvii) 1,8,27,64 . . . n. (n is the number of terms)

(xviii) x+2/x+x/3+4/x . . . n terms.

```java
import java.io.*;
public class Series18
{
        public static void main(String args[])throws
        IOException
        {
                int n, x;
                double sum=0;
                BufferedReader br=new BufferedReader(new
                InputStreamReader(System.in));
                System.out.println("Enter the value of x and
                n");
                x= Integer.parseInt(br.readLine());
                n=Integer.parseInt(br.readLine());
                for(int i=1;i<=n;i++)
                {
                    if(i%2!=0)
                            sum+=x/i;
                    else
                            sum+=i/x;
                }
                System.out.println("The sum is: "+sum);
        }
}
```

Input: x=2,n=3
Output: The sum is: 3.66

CHAPTER 6

PATTERN PRINTING

Programs At a Glance

➢ Program to print the following patterns:

(i) 1
   11
   111
   1111
   11111

(ii) 1
   12
   123
   1234
   12345

(iii) 1
   22
   333
   4444
   55555

(iv)
   45
   345
   2345
   12345

(v) 5
   44
   333
   2222
   11111

(vi) 11111
   2222
   333
   44
   5

(vii) 12345
1234
123
12
1

54321
4321
321
21
1

(ix) 55555
4444
333
22
1

(x) 54321
4321
321
21
1

(xi) 12345
2345
345
45
5

(xii) 55555
4444
333
22
1

(xiii)   1
21
321
4321
54321

(xiv)   1
22
333
4444
55555

(xv)   5
5
345
2345
12345

(xvi) 12345
12344
12333
12222
11111

(xvii) 54321
44321
33321
22221
11111

(viii) 11111
12222
12333
12344
12345

(xix)
```
          *
        *
      *
    *
  *
```

(xx)
```
*
  *
    *
      *
        *
```

(xxi)
```
* * * * * *
*         *
*         *
* * * * * *
```

(xxii)
```
* * * * * * * * * *
*                 *
* * * * * * * * * *
```

(xxiv)
```
    1
   111
  11111
 1111111
111111111
```

(xxv)
```
    1
   121
  12321
 1234321
123454321
```

(xxvi)
```
        *
      * * *
    * * * * *
  * * * * * * *
```

6.1 INTRODUCTION

You would have seen a lot of number based or symbol based patterns in your life. Pattern programming is rather a simple task but some simple minute changes in the source code can really affect the pattern. Let's see the variety of the patterns and their source codes.

PROGRAMMING EXAMPLES

Ques.6 Write a program to print the following patterns:

(iv)   1
       11
       111
       1111
       11111

```
public class Pattern1
{
    public static void main(String args[])
    {
        for(int i=1;i<=5;i++)
        {
            for(int j=1;j<=i;j++)
                System.out.print("1");
            System.out.println();
        }
    }
}
```

> **Note:**
>
> The pattern is analyzed as follows:
>
>   **inner loop (j)**
>
>   1 ———————
>   11
>   **outer loop (i)** 111
>   1111
>   11111
>
> The outer loop determines the number of rows while the inner loop determines the changing values.

(v)   1
            12
            123
            1234
            12345

```java
public class Pattern2
{
        public static void main(String args[])
        {
                for(int i=1;i<=5;i++)
                {
                        for(int j=1;j<=i;j++)
                        {
                                System.out.print(j);
                        }
                        System.out.println();
                }
        }
}
```

(vi)   1
    22
    333
    4444
    55555

```java
public class Pattern3
{
    public static void main(String args[])
    {
        for(int i=1;i<=5;i++)
        {
            for(int j=1;j<=i;j++)
            {
                System.out.print(i);
            }
            System.out.println();
        }
    }
}v
```

Practice Question

(iv) 5
   45
   345
   2345
   12345

(v) 5
   44
   333
   2222
   11111

```java
public class Pattern5
{
    public static void main(String args[])
```

```
    {
            for(int i=5;i>=1;i--)
            {
                    for(int j=i;j<=5;j++)
                    {
                            System.out.print(i);
                    }
                    System.out.println();
            }
        }
}
```

(vi)   **11111**
          2222
           333
            44
             5

```
public class Pattern6
{
        public static void main(String args[])
        {
                for(int i=1;i<=5;i++)
                {
                        for(int j=i;j<=5;j++)
                        {
                                System.out.print(i);
                        }
                        System.out.println();
                }
        }
}
```

(vii)   **12345**
          1234
          123
          12
          1

```
public class Pattern7
{
    public static void main(String args[])
    {
        for(int i=5;i>=1;i--)
        {
            for(int j=1;j<=i;j++)
            {
                System.out.print(j);
            }
            System.out.println();
        }
    }
}
```

(viii)   54321
       4321
       321
       21
       1

```
public class Pattern8
{
    public static void main(String args[])
    {
        for(int i=5;i>=1;i--)
        {
            for(int j=i;j>=1;j--)
            {
                System.out.print(j);
            }
            System.out.println();
        }
    }
}
```

Practice Question

(ix)   55555
        4444
        333
        22
        1

(x)   54321
          4321
           321
            21
             1


```java
public class Pattern10
{
        public static void main(String args[])
        {
                int sp=0;
                for(int i=5;i>=1;i--)
                {
                        for(int k=0;k<sp;k++)
                                System.out.print(" ");
                        for(int j=i;j>=1;j--)
                        {
                                System.out.print(j);
                        }
                        sp++;
                        System.out.println();
                }
        }
}
```

(xi)　12345
　　　　2345
　　　　　345
　　　　　　45
　　　　　　　5

```java
public class Pattern11
{
        public static void main(String args[])
        {
                int sp=0;
                for(int i=1;i<=5;i++)
                {
                        for(int k=0;k<sp;k++)
                                System.out.print(" ");
                        for(int j=i;j<=5;j++)
                        {
                                System.out.print(j);
                        }
                        sp++;
                        System.out.println();
                }
        }
}
```

Practice Question

(xii)   55555
           4444
            333
              22
                1

(xiii) 1
       21
      321
     4321
    54321

```
public class Pattern13
{
        public static void main(String args[])
        {
                int sp=4;
                for(int i=1;i<=5;i++)
                {
                        for(int k=0;k<sp;k++)
                                System.out.print(" ");
                        for(int j=i;j>=1;j--)
                        {
                                System.out.print(j);
                        }
                        sp--;
                        System.out.println();
                }
        }
}
```

(xiv)   1
              22
             333
            4444
           55555

```
public class Pattern14
{
        public static void main(String args[])
        {
                int sp=4;
                for(int i=1;i<=5;i++)
                {
                        for(int k=0;k<sp;k++)
                                System.out.print(" ");
                        for(int j=i;j>=1;j--)
                        {
                                System.out.print(i);
                        }
                        sp--;
                        System.out.println();
                }
        }
}
```

Practice Question

(xv)   5
         45
        345
       2345
      12345

(xvi)   **12345**
         12344
         12333
         12222
         11111

```
public class Pattern16
{
      public static void main(String args[])
      {
            for(int i=5;i>=1;i--)
            {
                  for(int j=1;j<i;j++)
                  {
                        System.out.print(j);
                  }
                  for(int k=i;k<=5;k++)
                  {
                        System.out.print(i);
                  }
                  System.out.println();
            }
      }
}
```

(xvii) 54321
44321
33321
22221
11111

```
public class Pattern17
{
        public static void main(String args[])
        {
                for(int i=5;i>=1;i--)
                {
                        for(int j=i;j<=5;j++)
                        {
                                System.out.print(i);
                        }
                        for(int k=(i-1);k>=1;k--)
                        {
                                System.out.print(k);
                        }
                        System.out.println();
                }
        }
}
```

Practice Question

(viii)   11111
           12222
           12333
           12344
           12345

(xix)
```
        *
      *
    *
  *
*
```

```java
public class Pattern
{
    public static void main(String args[])
    {
        for(int i=5;i>=1;i--)
        {
            for(int j=1;j<i;j++)
                System.out.print(" ");
            System.out.println("*");
        }
    }
}
```

(xx)　　*
　　　　　*
　　　　　　*
　　　　　　　*
　　　　　　　　*

```
public class Pattern
{
    public static void main(String args[])
    {
        for(int i=1;i<=5;i++)
        {
            System.out.println("*");
            for(int j=1;j<=i;j++)
                System.out.print(" ");
        }
    }
}
```

Practice Question

(xxi)
```
* * * * *
*       *
*       *
* * * * *
```

(xxii)
```
* * * * * * * * *
*               *
* * * * * * * * *
```

(xxiv)
```
        1
       111
      11111
     1111111
    111111111
```

```java
public class Pattern
{
    public static void main(String args[])
    {
        int i, j, k, l;
        for(i=1;i<=5;i++)
        {
            for(j=5;j>=i;j--)
                System.out.print(" ");
            for(k=1;k<=i;k++)
                System.out.print("1");
            for(l=k-2;l>0;l--)
                System.out.print("1");
            System.out.println(" ");
        }
    }
}
```

(xxv)
```
        1
       121
      12321
     1234321
    123454321
```

```java
public class Pattern
{
    public static void main(String args[])
    {
        int i, j, k, l;
        for(i=1;i<=5;i++)
        {
            for(j=5;j>=i;j--)
                System.out.print(" ");
            for(k=1;k<=i;k++)
                System.out.print(k);
            for(l=k-2;l>0;l--)
                System.out.print(l);
            System.out.println(" ");
        }
    }
}
```

Practice Question

(xxvi)
```
      *
    * * *
  * * * * *
* * * * * * *
```

CHAPTER 7

FUNCTIONS

- Concept of functions
- Use of Functions
- Call by Value
- Call by Reference
- Use of the return statement
- Recursion
- Constructors

Programs at a Glance

- Program to enter two numbers and add them. Make use of functions as per the requirement.
- Program to a number and check if it is prime or not.
- Program to enter five numbers and check which is prime.
- Program to enter five numbers and print the square of each of it. (Make a user defined function which returns the square of a number)
- Program to enter a number and check if it is automorphic or not.
- Program to enter a number and check if it is kaprekar or not.
- Program to input a number and test whether it is a magic number or not.
- Program to input a number and test whether it is a unique number or not.
- Program to swap two values using call by value.
- Program to swap two values using call by reference.
- Program that explains call by value.
- Program that explains call by reference.
- Program that returns the absolute value of a number.

Recursion

- Program to find the factorial of a number.
- Program to find the sum of first n natural numbers.
- Program to find the GCD of two numbers.
- Program to generate the Fibonacci series of first n numbers.

7.1 INTRODUCTION

Before going into the details of functions, let's know its basic meaning. Function means **to perform**. Functions are all around us in our daily life. For example, the function of a student is to study, the function of a worker is to his job, the function of a labor is to construct, etc. So in simple words we can say that a function is anything that performs a particular operation.

Note: A function is a group of statements which is able to perform a self-independent operation.

Functions are basically of two types:

(i) pre-defined functions

These are the functions which are already written in the compiler and we can use them as and when required.

Eg: **parseInt()** is a function which is used to convert the input into an integer.

indexOf(char) is a function which returns the index of a particular character in the string.

(ii) user-defined functions

These are the functions which are defined and written by the programmer as per the use. They may perform any kind of an operation depending upon how they are coded.

The major use of functions is to divide the code into individual fragments that enhances the readability of the program and also ensures easy debugging.

Eg: If a program is divided into functions and for suppose an error occurs, then we know that which part is the error generating code and so we can directly correct it rather than the scrutiny of the whole program.

7.2 WORKING WITH FUNCTIONS

When we need to execute the statements in a function we need to call that function. When we call a function it means we are asking the compiler to start executing the statements inside the function block. A function is can be called by three techniques:

Case 1: A function called by another function

Eg:

```
public void add()
{
        getInput();
        c=a+b;
        System.out.println("The sum is: "+c);
}
public void getInput()
{
        a=sc.nextInt();
        b=sc.nextInt();
}
```

add() is the calling function and getInput() is the called function.

Now let us see what exactly happens when a function is being called by another function.

```
public void func1()
{
        statement 1;
        func2();
        statement 4;
}
public void func2()
{
        statement 2;
        statement 3;
}
```

Firstly, statement 1 gets executed. Now when a call is made the func2() the compiler skips the remaining statements in func1() and executed func2(). After all the statements in func2() have executed successfully, the compiler goes back immediately to the next statement from where the call was made to func2(). And then the remaining statements in func1() re executed.

Case 2: A function called by the object

```
Eg:
public class abc
{
        public static void main(String args[])
        {
                abc obj=new abc();
                obj.name();
                System.out.println("Nicolas");
        }
        public void name()
        {
                System.out.println("Mark");
        }
}
```

In the above example, obj is the object of the class abc. When a call is made to the function name() then the compiler prints 'Mark' and then the control is transferred back to the statement immediately after from where the call was made, so the compiler print 'Nicolas'.

Case 3: A function calling itself

```
Eg:
        public int sum(int num)
        {
                if(num==1)
                        return 1;
                return(num+sum(num-1));
        }
```

The process is called as recursion. It is discussed in detail later in the chapter.

7.3 PASSING ARGUMENTS

In some cases, a function may require a particular value or a set of values to compute the operation. So these values have to be passed to the function at the time of calling.

Eg:

```java
import java.util.*;
public class Add
{
    public static void main(String args[])
    {
        int a, b;
        Scanner sc=new Scanner(System.in);
        a=sc.nextInt();
        b=sc.nextInt();
        sum(a, b);
    }
    public void sum(int x, int y)
    {
        int sum=x+y;
        System.out.println("The sum is:" +sum);
    }
}
```

In the above program first the console will ask to enter the values of a and b and then the sum will be displayed.

The function sum() computes the sum of two numbers, so it needs those two values as arguments.

If you notice when a call is made to the function [sum(a, b)], the two values are passed as a and b. These values are called actual arguments.

Now when the function is being declared, it is written as sum(int x, int y). Here x and y are formal arguments. 'x' gets the value of 'a' and 'y' gets the value of 'b'.

> **Note: Any change made in the formal arguments will not reflect in the actual arguments.**

7.4 RETURNING A VALUE

In the above program if you notice **void** is written in the definition of the function sum(). It means that the function is not returning any value. But what if we want a function to return some value like any integer, float, etc.? In such cases the return type of the function has to be defined in the function definition.

Eg: Consider the program to add two numbers.

```
import java.util.*;
public class Add
{
        public static void main(String args[])
        {
                int a, b, c;
                Scanner sc=new Scanner(System.in);
                a=sc.nextInt();
                b=sc.nextInt();
                c=sum(a, b);
        }
        public int sum(int x, int y)
        {
                int sum=x+y;
                return sum;
        }
}
```

In this program the function sum() returns an integer type value. So when the function sum() is called it will also return some value. In this case, the function returns the sum of two numbers. As soon as the return statement is encountered, the value is returned and the function gets terminated.

> **Note: A function may have multiple return statements but it can return only one value. As and when the first return statement gets executed, the function gets terminated.**

PROGRAMMING EXAMPLES

Ques.7.1 Write a program to enter two numbers and add them. Make use of functions as per the requirement.

```
import java.io.*;
public class Add
{
        int a, b;
        public void getData()throws IOException
        {
                BufferedReader br=new BufferedReader(new
                InputStreamReader(System.in));
                System.out.println("Enter two numbers");
                a=Integer.parseInt(br.readLine());
                b=Integer.parseInt(br.readLine());
        }
        public void sum()
        {
                int sum=a+b;
                System.out.println("The sum is: "+sum);
        }
        public static void main(String args[])throws
        IOException
        {
                Add obj=new Add();
                obj.getData();
                obj.sum();
        }
}
```

Ques.7.2 **Write a program to a number and check if it is prime or not.**

```
import java.io.*;
public class Prime
{
        int n;
        public void getData()throws IOException
        {
                BufferedReader br=new BufferedReader(new
                InputStreamReader(System.in));
                System.out.println("Enter a number");
                n=Integer.parseInt(br.readLine());
        }
        public void prime()
        {
            int c=0;
            for(int i=1;i<=n;i++)
            {
                    if(n%i==0)
                    c++;
            }
            if(c==2)
                    System.out.println("It is a prime number");
            else
                    System.out.println("It is not a prime number");
        }
        public static void main(String args[])throws
        IOException
        {
                Prime obj=new Prime();
                obj.getData();
                obj.prime();
        }
}
```

Ques.7.3 Write a program to enter five numbers and check which is prime.

```java
import java.io.*;
public class Prime1
{
        int n;
        public void getData()throws IOException
        {
                BufferedReader br=new BufferedReader(new
                InputStreamReader(System.in));
                System.out.println("Enter a number");
                n=Integer.parseInt(br.readLine());
        }
        public void prime()throws IOException
        {
                int c;
                for(int i=1;i<=5;i++)
                {
                    c=0;
                    getData();
                    for(int j=i;j<=n;j++)
                    {
                        if(n%j==0)
                        c++;
                    }
                    if(c==2)
                        System.out.println(n+" is a prime number");
                    else
                        System.out.println(n+" is not a prime number");
                }
        }
        public static void main(String args[])throws
        IOException
        {
                Prime1 obj=new Prime1();
                obj.prime();
        }
}
```

Practice Question

Ques.7.4 Write a program to enter five numbers and print the square of each of it. (Make a user defined function which returns the square of a number)

Ques.7.5 Write a program to enter a number and check if it is automorphic or not.

> Automorphic numbers include numbers like:
> 5,25,etc.
> 5*5=25
> 25*25=625

```java
import java.io.*;
public class Automorphic
{
        int num, temp, c=0,n;
        public void getInput()throws IOException
        {
                BufferedReader br=new BufferedReader(new
                InputStreamReader(System.in));
                System.out.println("Enter a number");
                num=Integer.parseInt(br.readLine());
        }
        public int check()
        {
                n=num*num;
                temp=num;
                while(temp>0)
                {
                        c++;
                        temp=temp/10;
                }
                if(n%Math.pow(10,c)==num)
                        return 1;
                        return 0;
        }
        public static void main(String args[])throws
        IOException
        {
                Automorphic obj=new Automorphic();
                obj.getInput();
                int n=obj.check();
```

```java
        if(n==1)
                System.out.println("Automorphic");
        else
                System.out.println("Not Automorphic");
    }
}
```

Practice Question

Ques.7.6 Write a program to enter a number and check if it is kaprekar or not.

> Kaprekar number are the number which exhibit the following nature:
> 9*9=81 . . . Now 8+1=9.
> 45*45=2025 . . . Now 20+25=45

Ques.7.7 Write a program to input a number and test whether it is a magic number or not.

> ➤ Magic numbers are those numbers in which if we recursively keep on making the sum of the digits then the sum is 1.

```
import java.io.*;
public class Magic
{
        int num;
        public void getInput()throws IOException
        {
                BufferedReader br=new BufferedReader(new
                InputStreamReader(System.in));
                System.out.println("Enter a number");
                num=Integer.parseInt(br.readLine());
        }
        public int check()
        {
                int r, s=0;
                while(true)
                {
                        while(num>0)
                        {
                                r=num%10;
                                s=s+r;
                                num=num/10;
                        }
                        if(s>=0 && s<=9)
                        {
                                if(s==1)
                                        return 1;
                                else
                                        return 0;
                        }
                        else
                        {
                                num=s;
```

```
                s=0;
            }
        }
    }
public static void main(String args[])throws
IOException
    {
        Magic obj=new Magic();
        obj.getInput();
        int c=obj.check();
        if(c==1)
                System.out.println("It is a Magic number");
        else
                System.out.println("It is not a Magic number");

    }
}
```

Practice Question

Ques.7.8 Write a program to input a number and test whether it is a unique number or not.

Ques.7.9 Write a program to swap two values using call by value.

```java
import java.util.*;
public class Value
{
        static int a, b;
        public void getData()
        {
                Scanner sc=new Scanner(System.in);
                System.out.println("Enter two numbers");
                a=sc.nextInt();
                b=sc.nextInt();
        }
        public void swap(int c, int d)
        {
                System.out.println("Before swapping the valuev
                of a is "+a+" and b is "+b);
                c=c+d;
                d=c-d;
                c=c-d;
                System.out.println("After swapping the value
                of a is "+a+" and b is "+b);
        }
        public static void main(String args[])
        {
                Value obj=new Value();
                obj.getData();
                obj.swap(a, b);
        }
}
```

Program Analysis:

Suppose a=2, b=3.
The output of the above code is:

Before swapping the value of a and b is 2 and 3.
After swapping the value of a and b is 2 and 3.

So its quite clear the value has not been swapped.

The reason to this is, when we use call be value then a separate copy of the variable is created which has no affect on the original copy.

In the above program 'c' is a copy of 'a' and 'd' is the copy of 'b'. But any change made in c will not reflect in a and any change made in 'd' will not reflect in 'b'.

> **Input: a=5,b=6**
> **Output: a=5, b=6**

Ques.7.10 Write a program to swap two values using call by reference.

```java
import java.util.*;
public class Reference
{
    static int a, b;
    public void getData()
    {
        Scanner sc=new Scanner(System.in);
        System.out.println("Enter two numbers");
        a=sc.nextInt();
        b=sc.nextInt();
    }
    public void swap(Value obj1)
    {
        System.out.println("Before swapping the value
        of a is "+obj1.a+" and b is "+obj1.b);
        obj1.a=obj1.a+obj1.b;
        obj1.b=obj1.a-obj1.b;
        obj1.a=obj1.a-obj1.b;
        System.out.println("After swapping the value
        of a is "+obj1.a+" and b is "+obj1.b);
    }
    public static void main(String args[])
    {
        Reference obj=new Reference();
        obj.getData();
        obj.swap(obj);
    }
}
```

Program Analysis:

Suppose a=2, b=3.
The output of the above code is:

Before swapping the value of a and b is 2 and 3.
After swapping the value of a and b is 3 and 2.

So that the values have been swapped.

In this case we are not making use of any other variable to store the copy. Rather we are giving the reference to both the variables.

So any change made two the reference copies, will affect the value of variables as well.

> **Input: a=5,b=6**
> **Output: a=6, b=5**

Practice Question

Ques.7.11 Write a program that explains call by value.

Ques.7.12 Write a program that explains call by reference.

Ques.7.13 **Write a program that returns the absolute value of a number.**

```java
import java.io.*;
public class Number
{
        int num;
        public void getInput()throws IOException
        {
                BufferedReader br=new BufferedReader(new
                InputStreamReader(System.in));
                System.out.println("Enter a number");
                num=Integer.parseInt(br.readLine());
        }
        public int absolute()
        {
                int n=num;
                if(n<0)
                n*=-1;
                return n;
        }
        public static void main(String args[])throws IOException
        {
                Number obj=new Number();
                obj.getInput();
                int n=obj.absolute();
                System.out.println("The absolute is:"+n);
        }
}
```

7.5 RECURSION

A function calling itself is called recursion or we can say that calling a function in its definition is called recursion. Now you might be wondering that when a function will always call itself, then it will create an infinite cycle. However we can break this flow of execution using the return statement. To end our loop, we can check if a particular condition is true and in that case we can exit the method.

Programming Examples

Ques.7.14 Write a program to find the factorial of a number.

```
import java.util.*;
public class Factorial
{
        public void main(String args[])
        {
                Scanner sc=new Scanner(System.in);
                int n;
                System.out.println("Enter a number");
                n=sc.nextInt();
                int f=fact(n);
                System.out.println("The factorial is: "+f);
        }
        public int fact(int num)
        {
                if(num==1)
                        return 1;
                return(num*fact(num-1));
        }
}
```

Program Analysis:

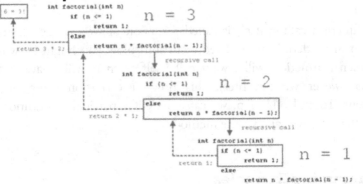

```
Input: num=4
Output: The factorial is: 24
```

Ques.7.15 Write a program to find the sum of first n natural numbers.

```java
import java.util.*;
public class Add
{
        public void main(String args[])
        {
                Scanner sc=new Scanner(System.in);
                int n, s;
                System.out.println("Enter a number");
                n=sc.nextInt();
                s=sum(n);
                System.out.println("The sum is: "+s);
        }
        public int sum(int num)
        {
                if(num==1)
                        return 1;
                return(num+sum(num-1));
        }
}
```

```
Input: num=5
Output: The sum is: 15
```

Ques.7.16 Write a program to find the GCD of two numbers.

```java
import java.util.*;
public class Divisor
{
        public void main(String args[])
        {
                Scanner sc=new Scanner(System.in);
                int n1,n2,gcd;
                System.out.println("Enter two numbers");
                n1=sc.nextInt();
                n2=sc.nextInt();
                gcd=GCD(n1,n2);
                System.out.println("The gcd is: "+gcd);
        }
        public int GCD(int n1,int n2)
        {
                int rem;
                rem=n1%n2;
                if(rem==0)
                        return n2;
                else
                return(GCD(n2,rem));
        }
}
```

> Input: n1=3, n2=9
> Output: The gcd is: 3

Practice Question

Ques.7.18 Write a program to enter two numbers and find their LCM.

Ques.7.17 **Write a program to generate the Fibonacci series of first n numbers.**

```java
import java.util.*;
public class Fibo
{
        public void main(String args[])
        {
                Scanner sc=new Scanner(System.in);
                int n;
                System.out.println("Enter a number");
                n=sc.nextInt();
                for(int i=0;i<n;i++)
                System.out.print(fibonacci(i));
        }
        public int fibonacci(int i)
        {
                if(i<=2)
                        return 1;
                else
                return(fibonacci(i-1)+fibonacci(i-2));
        }
}
```

7.6 CONSTRUCTORS

Constructor is a block of code which is executed when an object is created. Unlike functions, constructors have the same name as that of the class, with no return type. They are used to initialize the objects with legal initial values.

There are two types of constructors:

(i) Non-Parameterized Constructors

Non-parameterized constructors often called as default constructor is automatically made by the compiler upon the execution of the program or they can also be declared explicitly.

Eg: Consider the following example:

```
public class Number
{
        int a, b, c;
        public void output()
        {
                System.out.println("a= "+a);
                System.out.println("b= "+b);
                System.out.println("c= "+c);
        }
        public void main(String args[])
        {
                Number obj=new Number();
                obj.output();
        }
}
```

The output of the above piece of code is:
a=0
b=0
c=0

The same code is written below, but here we have explicitly defined a default constructor.

```
public class Number
{
        int a, b, c;
        Number()
        {
                a=0;
                b=0;
                c=0;
        }
        public void output()
        {
                System.out.println("a= "+a);
                System.out.println("b= "+b);
```

```
            System.out.println("c= "+c);
    }
    public void main(String args[])
    {
            Number obj=new Number();
            obj.output();
    }
}
```

The output of this code is:

a=0

b=0

c=0

Note: The default constructor has the same name as that of the class and has not return type, not even void.

(ii) Parameterized Constructor

Such constructors are used to initialize the data members with their initial values when an object to their class is created.

Eg:

```
public class Number
{
    int a, b, c;
    Number(int x, int y, int z)
    {
            a=x;
            b=y;
            c=z;
    }
    public void output()
    {
            System.out.println("a= "+a);
            System.out.println("b= "+b);
            System.out.println("c= "+c);
    }
```

```
public static void main(String args[])
{
        Number obj=new Number(2,3,4);
        obj.output();
}
}
```

> When an object obj is created for the class Number then automatically the values are assigned to the respective data members a, b and c.

7.7 QUESTION HOUR

(i)   Why are functions used?

(ii) Explain the difference between user-defined and pre-defined function.

(iii) Explain any two pre-defined functions in detail.

(iv) What is the difference between call by value and call by reference?

(v)   Explain recursion.

(vi) Is recursion faster than looping? How?

(vii) What is a constructor?

(viii) What is the difference between a parameterized and non-parameterized constructor?

CHAPTER 8

INTRODUCTION TO ARRAYS

- Concept of Arrays
- Memory Allocation of arrays
- Single-dimensional arrays
- Double-dimensional arrays
- Programming Examples
- Practice Questions
- Multiple-choice questions

Programs At a Glance

- Program to input an array of 10 elements and then display it.
- Program to input an array of 10 elements and print it in reverse order.
- Program to input an array and create a copy of that array.
- Program to input an array and find the mean of its elements.
- Program to input an array and find the sum of even and odd numbers separately.
- Program to initialize two arrays and store their sum in a third array.
- Program to 0 elements in an array and find the maximum and the minimum element of the array.
- Program to calculate the number of days in a year using arrays.
- Program to input an array, then store all the positive elements in another array.
- Program to enter an array and find the positon of the largest element in the array.
- Program and check if it contains a duplicate element.
- Program to print the frequency of each element of an array.
- Program to store the first 15 elements of the Fibonacci series in an array.
- Program to insert a number in the middle of an array.
- Program to delete an element from the array.
- Program to replace an element in the array.
- Program to input a 3X3 matrix and display it.
- Program to enter two matrices and find their sum.
- Program to enter a 2X3 matrix and a 3X2 matrix and find their sum.
- Program to enter two matrices and find their product.
- Program to find the transpose of a matrix.
- Program to enter a matrix and check if it is an identity matrix.
- Program to enter a 4X4 matrix and find the sum of right and the left diagonals.
- Program to enter a matrix and find the sum of each row and column.
- Program to enter a 4X4 matrix and find the sum of its boundary elements.
- Program to enter a date and check if it is a valid date.
- Program to enter a date and print the corresponding day on that date.

8.1 INTRODUCTION

An array is used when we have to process a large amount of data. Eg: When we have to enter marks of 50 students then we cannot take 50 independent variables. We need a powerful data type which can handle large amount of data efficiently.

An array is a fixed-sized sequenced collection of elements of the same data type or in other words an array is a collection of variables of the same data type that are referred by a common name.

Java offers different types of arrays:

 (i) One-Dimensional Arrays
 (ii) Two-Dimensional Arrays
 (iii) Multi-Dimensional Arrays

8.2 ONE-DIMENSIONAL ARRAY

It is the simplest form of an array. The array is given a name and its elements are referred to by their subscripts or indices. The index numbering starts from 0.

The general form of declaration is:

type variable_name[size];

The 'type' specifies the type of the elements the array will hold and the 'size' decides the number of elements the array will hold.

Eg:
  int a[10];

It will create an array with the name a which can store 10 integer elements.

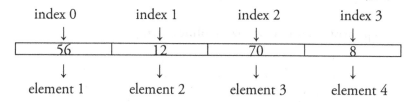

Each element is assigned an index. The value of the last index is always one less than the size of the array. Since the index number is unique so each and every element of the array can be accessed separately.

An array can be initialized in two ways:

(i) Compile Time
(ii) Run Time

Compile Time Initialization

The general form of initialization of a 1-D array is:

type array_name[size]={ list of values };

Eg: int number[3]={ 1,2,3 };

This will create an array 'number' with size '3' and these elements will be stored in it.

Run Time Initialization

An array can also be initialized at the run time.
Eg: int x[3];
        for(int i=0;i<3;i++)
          x[i]=sc.nextInt();

This will initialize the values to the array as per the users choice.

8.3 TWO-DIMENSIONAL ARRAYS

Two Dimension arrays are declared as follows:

type array_name[row_size][column_size];

'Array_name' is the name of the array, 'type' is the base type of the array, 'row_size' is the number of rows and 'column_size' is the number of columns in the array.

Eg:
int arr[2][3] ;

It will create an with the name arr which will contain 2 rows and 3 columns.

a[0][0]	a[0][1]	a[0][2]	a[0][3]
a[1][0]	a[1][1]	a[1][2]	a[1][3]
a[2][0]	a[2][1]	a[2][2]	a[2][3]

Each and very cell is identified by a row and a column number. The first bracket contains the row number and the second bracket has the column number.

A 2-D array can be initialized in two ways:

(i) Compile Time
(ii) Run Time

Compile Time Initialization

At the compile time an array can be initialized as:

int a[][]={{1,2,3},{4,5,6},{7,8,9}} where the internal braces represent rows independently.

Run Time Initialization

At the run time we can assign values to an array like:

```
int arr[2][3];
for(int i=0;i<2;i++)
        for(int j=0;j<3;j++)
        arr[i][j]=sc.nextInt();
```

This will initialize the values as per the user's choice.

PROGRAMMING EXAMPLES

Ques.8.1 Write a program to input an array of 10 elements and then display it.

```
import java.io.*;
public class Display
{
intarr[]=new int[10];
        public void getInput()throws IOException
        {
                BufferedReaderbr=new BufferedReader(new
                InputStreamReader(System.in));
                System.out.println("Enter 10 elements in the array");
                        for(int i=0;i<10;i++)
                        arr[i]=Integer.parseInt(br.readLine());
        }
        public void display()
        {
                System.out.println("The elements you entered are:");
                        for(int i=0;i<10;i++)
                        System.out.print(arr[i]+"\t");
        }
```

```
public static void main(String args[])throws
IOException
{
    Display obj=new Display();
    obj.getInput();
    obj.display();
}
}
```

Note:

Blank Array . . .

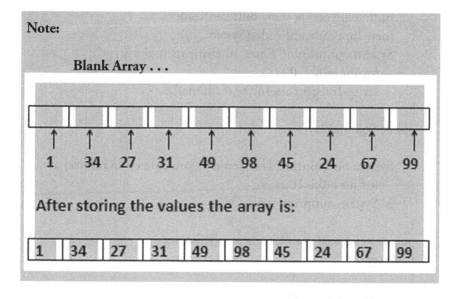

After storing the values the array is:

| 1 | 34 | 27 | 31 | 49 | 98 | 45 | 24 | 67 | 99 |

Ques.8.2 Write a program to input an array of 10 elements and print it in reverse order.

```java
import java.io.*;
public class Reverse
{
intarr[]=new int[10];
    public void getInput()throws IOException
    {
        BufferedReaderbr=new BufferedReader
        (new InputStreamReader(System.in));
        System.out.println("Enter 10 elements in the array");
            for(int i=0;i<10;i++)
            arr[i]=Integer.parseInt(br.readLine());
    }
    public void display()
    {
        System.out.println("The elements you entered(in reverse) are:");
            for(int i=0;i<10;i++)
            System.out.print(arr[i]+"\t");
    }
    public static void main(String args[])throws
    IOException
    {
        Reverse obj=new Reverse();
        obj.getInput();
        obj.display();

    }
}
```

Practice Question

Ques.8.3 Write a program to input an array and create a copy of that array.

Ques.8.4 Write a program to input an array and find the mean of its elements.

```java
import java.util.*;
public class SumAver
{
    intarr[]=new int[10];
    int sum;
    double avg;
    public void getInput()
    {
        Scanner sc=new Scanner(System.in);
        System.out.println("Enter 10 elements in the array");
        for(int i=0;i<10;i++)
            arr[i]=sc.nextInt();
    }
    public void compute()
    {
        sum=0;
        for(int i=0;i<10;i++)
            sum+=arr[i];
        avg=sum/10.0;
    }
    public void display()
    {
        System.out.println("The sum is: "+sum);
        System.out.println("The average is: "+avg);
    }
    public static void main(String args[])
    {
        SumAverobj=new SumAver();
        obj.getInput();
        obj.compute();
        obj.display();
    }
}
```

arr[]={5,64,53,42,45,23,12,45,5, 78}
The mean is: 37.2

Ques.8.5 Write a program to input an array and find the sum of even and odd numbers separately.

```java
import java.io.*;
public class EvenOdd
{
intarr[]=new int[10];
intsum_even=0,sum_odd=0;
    public void getInput()throws IOException
    {
        BufferedReaderbr=new BufferedReader(new
        InputStreamReader(System.in));
        System.out.println("Enter 10 elements in the array");
        for(int i=0;i<10;i++)
            arr[i]=Integer.parseInt(br.readLine());
    }
    public void calc()
    {
        for(int i=0;i<10;i++)
        {
            if(arr[i]%2==0)
                sum_even+=arr[i];
            else
                sum_odd+=arr[i];
        }
    }
    public void display()
    {
        System.out.println("The sum of even numbers is: "+sum_even);
        System.out.println("The sum of odd numbers is: "+sum_odd);
    }
    public static void main(String args[])throws IOException
    {
        EvenOdd obj=new EvenOdd();
        obj.getInput();
        obj.calc();
        obj.display();
    }
}
```

```
arr[]={5,64,53,42,45,23,12,45,5, 78}
The sum of even numbers is:196
The sum of odd numbers is:176
```

Practice Question

Ques.8.6 Write a program to initialize two arrays and store their sum in a third array.

Ques.8.7 Write a program to enter 5 elements in an array and store the factorial of its elements in another array.

Ques.8.8 Write a program to input 10 elements in an array and find the maximum and the minimum element of the array.

```java
import java.util.*;
public class MaxMin
{
    int arr[]=new int[10];
    public void getInput()
    {
        Scanner sc=new Scanner(System.in);
        System.out.println("Enter 10 elements in the array");
        for(int i=0;i<10;i++)
            arr[i]=sc.nextInt();
    }
    public void check()
    {
        int max=arr[0],min=arr[0];
        for(int i=0;i<10;i++)
        {
            if(arr[i]>max)
                max=arr[i];
            if(arr[i]<min)
                min=arr[i];
        }
        System.out.println("The maximum number is:"+max);
        System.out.println("The minimum number is:"+min);
    }
    public static void main(String args[])
    {
        MaxMin obj=new MaxMin();
        obj.getInput();
        obj.check();
    }
}
```

Ques.8.9 Write a program to calculate the number of days in a year using arrays.

```
import java.util.*;
public class Year
{
        public void display()
        {
        int yy, tdays=0;
        int days[]={31,28,31,30,31,30,31,31,30,31,30,31};
        Scanner sc=new Scanner(System.in);
        System.out.println("Enter a year");
        yy=sc.nextInt();
        if(yy%4==0)
            days[1]=29;
        for(int i=0;i<days.length;i++)
            tdays+=days[i];
        System.out.println("The total days are:"+tdays);
        }
        public static void main(String args[])
        {
            Year obj=new Year();
            obj.display();
        }
}
```

Ques.8.10 Write a program to input an array, then store all the positive elements in another array.

```java
import java.io.*;
public class Positive
{
int arr1[]=new int[10];
int arr2[]=new int[10];
int c=0;
        public void getInput()throws IOException
        {
            BufferedReaderbr=new BufferedReader(new
            InputStreamReader(System.in));
            System.out.println("Enter 10 elements in the array");
            for(int i=0;i<10;i++)
                arr1[i]=Integer.parseInt(br.readLine());
        }
        public void store()
        {
            for(int i=0;i<10;i++)
            {
                if(arr1[i]>0)
                arr2[c]=arr1[i];
                c++;
            }
        }
        public void display()
        {
            System.out.println("The positive elements the array are:");
            for(int i=0;i<c;i++)
            System.out.print(arr2[i]+"\t");
        }
        public static void main(String args[])throws IOException
        {
            Positive obj=new Positive();
            obj.getInput();
            obj.store();
            obj.display();
        }
}
```

Practice Question

Ques.8.11 Write a program to enter an array and find the positon of the largest element in the array.

Ques.8.12 **Write a program and check if it contains a duplicate element.**

```java
import java.io.*;
public class Duplicate
{
int arr[]=new int[10],flag=1;
    public void getInput()throws IOException
    {
        BufferedReaderbr=new BufferedReader(new
        InputStreamReader(System.in));
        System.out.println("Enter 10 elements in the array");
        for(int i=0;i<10;i++)
            arr[i]=Integer.parseInt(br.readLine());
    }
    public void dup()
    {
        for(int i=0;i<9;i++)
        {
            for(int j=i+1;j<10;j++)
            {
                if(arr[i]==arr[j])
                flag=0;
            }
        }
        if(flag==1)
            System.out.println("No Duplicate found");
        else
            System.out.println("Duplicate Found");
    }
    public static void main(String args[])throws IOException
    {
        Duplicate obj=new Duplicate();
        obj.getInput();
        obj.dup();
    }
}
```

Practice Question

Ques.8.13 Write a program to print the frequency of each element of an array.

Ques.8.14 Write a program to store the first 15 elements of the Fibonacci series in an array.

Ques.8.15 **Write a program to insert a number in the middle of an array.**

```java
import java.util.*;
public class Insert
{
        int arr[]=new int[10],pos, val;
        public void getInput()
        {
                Scanner sc=new Scanner(System.in);
                System.out.println("Enter 5 elements in the array");
                for(int i=0;i<5;i++)
                        arr[i]=sc.nextInt();
                System.out.println("Enter the value and
                position of the element");
                val=sc.nextInt();
                pos=sc.nextInt();
        }
        public void ins()
        {
                for(int i=5;i>=pos;i--)
                        arr[i+1]=arr[i];
                        arr[pos]=val;
        }
        public void display()
        {
                System.out.println("The new array is:");
                for(int i=0;i<10;i++)
                System.out.print(arr[i]+"\t");

        }
        public static void main(String args[])
        {
                Insert obj=new Insert();
                obj.getInput();
                obj.ins();
                obj.display();
        }
}
```

Ques.8.16 Write a program to delete an element from the array.

```java
import java.util.*;
public class Delete
{
    int arr[]=new int[10],pos;
    Scanner sc=new Scanner(System.in);
    public void getInput()
    {
        System.out.println("Enter 10 elements in the array");
        for(int i=0;i<10;i++)
            arr[i]=sc.nextInt();
    }
    public void del()
    {
        System.out.println("Enter the position");
        pos=sc.nextInt();
        for(int i=pos;i<9;i++)
            arr[i]=arr[i+1];
    }
    public void display()
    {
        System.out.println("The new array is:");
        for(int i=0;i<9;i++)
        System.out.print(arr[i]+"\t");
    }
    public static void main(String args[])
    {
        Delete obj=new Delete();
        obj.getInput();
        obj.del();
        obj.display();
    }
}
```

Practice Question

Ques.8.17 Write a program to replace an element in the array.

Ques.8.18 Write a program to input a 3X3 matrix and display it.

```
import java.io.*;
public class DisplayMatrix
{
int matrix[][]=new int[3][3];
    public void getInput()throws IOException
    {
        BufferedReaderbr=new BufferedReader(new
        InputStreamReader(System.in));
        System.out.println("Enter the elements");
        for(int i=0;i<3;i++)
        {
            for(int j=0;j<3;j++)
            matrix[i][j]=Integer.parseInt(br.readLine());
        }
    }
    public void display()
    {
        System.out.println("The matrix form is");
        for(int i=0;i<3;i++)
        {
            for(int j=0;j<3;j++)
            System.out.print(matrix[i][j]+"\t");
            System.out.println();
        }
    }
    public static void main(String args[])throws IOException
    {
        DisplayMatrixobj=new DisplayMatrix();
        obj.getInput();
        obj.display();
    }
}
```

Ques.8.19 Write a program to enter two matrices and find their sum.

```java
import java.util.*;
public class SumMatrix
{
int matrix1[][], matrix2[][], matrix3[][];
int m, n;
    public void getInput()
    {
            Scanner sc=new Scanner(System.in);
            System.out.println("Enter the size of the
            matrices");
            m=sc.nextInt();
            n=sc.nextInt();
            matrix1=new int[m][n];
            matrix2=new int[m][n];
            matrix3=new int[m][n];
            System.out.println("Enter the elements of the
            first matrix");
            for(int i=0;i<m;i++)
            {
                    for(int j=0;j<n;j++)
                    matrix1[i][j]=sc.nextInt();
            }
            System.out.println("Enter the matrix of the second matrix");
            for(int i=0;i<m;i++)
            {
                    for(int j=0;j<n;j++)
                    matrix2[i][j]=sc.nextInt();
            }
            public void add()
            {
                    System.out.println("After addition, the new matrix is");
                    for(int i=0;i<m;i++)
                    {
                            for(int j=0;j<n;j++)
                            matrix3[i][j]=matrix1[i][j]+matrix2[i][j];
                    }
            }
```

```
public void display()
{
        for(int i=0;i<m;i++)
        {
                for(int j=0;j<n;j++)
                System.out.print(matrix3[i][j]+"\t");
                System.out.println();
        }
}
public static void main(String args[])
{
        SumMatrixobj=new SumMatrix();
        obj.getInput();
        obj.add();
        obj.display();
}
}
```

Practice Question

Ques.8.20 Write a program to enter a 2X3 matrix and a 3X2 matrix and find their sum.

Ques.8.21 Write a program to enter two matrices and find their product.

Ques.8.22 Write a program to to enter numbers in a circular fashion (clockwise) with natural numbers in a square matrix.

```java
import java.util.*;
class circular
{
        public static void main (String[]args)
        {
                Scanner st = new Scanner (System.in);
                System.out.println("Enter size of matrix");
                int n = st.nextInt();
                int mat [][]= new int[n][n];
                int c1=0,c2=n-1,r1=0,r2=n-1;
                do
                {
                        for (int x = c1;x<=c2 ;x++ )
                        {
                                mat[0][x]=k;
                                k++;
                        }
                        for (int int y =r1+1;y<=r2 ;y++;)
                        {
                                mat[y][n-1]=k;
                                k++;
                        }
                        for (int x=c2-1;x>=c1 ;x-- )
                        {
                                mat[r2][x]=k;
                                k++;
                        }
                        for (int y = r2-1;y>=r1+1 ;y-- )
                        {
                                mat[y][c1]=k;
                                k++;
                        }
                        c1++;
                        c2--;
                        r1++;
                        r2--;
```

```
        }
        while (k<=n*n);
        System.out.println("Circular matrix is" -);
        for (int r = 0;r<4 ;r++ )
        {
                for (int c =0 ;c<4 ;c++ )
                {
                        System.out.print(mat[r][c]);
                }
                System.out.println();
        }
    }
}
```

Ques.8.23 Write a program to enter a month a print its calender.

```java
import java.io.*;
class q
{
public void main()throws IOException
{
    int sp, dd=1,mm=0,y=1900,f=1,n, s=0,pos=0;
    String b="";
    int d[]={31,28,31,30,31,30,31,31,30,31,30,31};
    String w[]={"monday","tuesday","wednesday","thursday","friday",
    "saturday","sunday"};
    String m[]={"jan","feb","mar","apr","may","june","july","aug","sept",
    "oct","nov","dec"};
    BufferedReader k=new BufferedReader(new
    InputStreamReader(System.in));
    for(int u=1;u<3;u++)
    {
        System.out.println("ENTER DATE--->");
        dd=Integer.parseInt(k.readLine());
        System.out.println("ENTER MONTH--->");
        mm=Integer.parseInt(k.readLine());
        System.out.println("ENTER YEAR--->");
        y=Integer.parseInt(k.readLine());
        System.out.println();
        int h=y;
        int yy=y;
        f=1;
        s=0;
        while(yy>=1900)
        {
            if(mm<13 && mm>0)
            {
                if(d[mm-1]>=dd && dd>0 )
                {
                    f=0;
                    if(h%4==0)
                    {
                        d[1]=29;
```

```java
            if(h==yy)
            {
                for(int i=0;i<=mm-2;i++)
                {
                    s=s+d[i];
                }
            }
        }
        else
        {
            d[1]=28;
            if(h==yy)
            {
                for(int o=0;o<=mm-2;o++)
                {
                    s=s+d[o];
                }
            }
            else
                {
                for(n=0;n<=11;n++)
                    {
                        s=s+d[n];
                    }
                }
            }
        }
    }
    else
    {
        f=1;
        break;
    }
        h--;
        yy--;
}
System.out.println();
if(f==0)
```

```java
{
  if(s>=0 && y>=1900)
  {
     sp=s%7;
     System.out.println("CALENDER OF "+" "+m[mm-1]+"
     "+"--->");
     System.out.println(" "+"Mon"+" "+"Tue"+" "+"Wed"+" "
     +"Thu"+" "+"Fri"+" "+"Sat"+" "+"Sun"+"");
     if(sp<7)
     {
        for(int sd=sp;sd>=1;sd--)
        {
            System.out.print(" "+" ");
        }
     }
     if(y%4==0)
        {
            d[1]=28;
        }
     else
        {
            d[1]=28;
        }
        int c=sp;
        for(int g=1;g<=d[mm-1];g++)
        {
          c++;
          System.out.print(g+" ");
          if(c%7==0)
          {
              System.out.println();
          }
            if(g==dd)
            {
                pos=g;
            }
        }
            int e=((pos+sp)%7);
            if(e==0)
```

```
            {
                b=w[6];
            }
        else
            {
                b=w[e-1];
            }
                System.out.println();
                System.out.println(b+" "+dd+" "+m[mm-1]+" "+y);
                System.out.println();
    }


    }
    if(f==1)
    {
        System.out.println("ENTER WRONG DATE");
    }
        System.out.println();
    }
}
}
```

Ques.8.24 Write a program to enter a date and check if it's a valid date or not.

8.4 QUESTION HOUR

(i)   What is the use of an array?

(ii)   What is the difference between one and two dimensional arrays?

(iii) Explain run-time initialization of an array.

(iv) Can we change the size of an array once declared?

(v)   Give any two major drawbacks of arrays.

(vi) Explain row major and column major wise allocation in an array.

(vii) Explain the concept of index in an array.

(viii) How can we determine the size of an array?

(ix) Can an array be a mixture of different data types?

CHAPTER 9

MANIPULATING STRINGS

- Strings
- String handling functions
- Programming Examples

Programs at a Glance

- ➤ Program to enter a string from the user and then display it.
- ➤ Program to enter a string and print its length.
- ➤ Program to input a string from the user and then display it in reverse order.
- ➤ Program to input a string and count the number of vowels and consonants in it.
- ➤ Program to enter a string and count the occurrence of each vowel.
- ➤ Program to input a string and print the frequency of each character.
- ➤ Program to enter a word and sort it in alphabetical order.
- ➤ Program to enter a string in lower case and convert it into upper case without using any in-built function.
- ➤ Program to enter two strings and print which is greater.
- ➤ Program to input a string and check if it is a palindrome.
- ➤ Program to input a string and insert a character at a particular positionprogram to enter a string and count the number of alphabets, digits and special characters in it.
- ➤ Program to enter a string and print each word in a separate line.
- ➤ Program to enter a string and print the number of words in it.
- ➤ Program to enter a string and count the occurrences of the word "the".
- ➤ Program to input a string and delete the occurrences of the word "the".
- ➤ Program to delete all the spaces in a sentence without using trim() function.
- ➤ Program to replace all the occurrences of the character 'a' with 'e'.
- ➤ Program to enter a sentence and make every the first letter of every word in upper case.
- ➤ Program to enter a name and print its initials.

9.1 INTRODUCTION

String is nothing but sequence of characters. Eg: A name is string, a phone number, your address are all strings.

A String may be a combination of alphabets, integers and special symbols.

Eg: "abc", "abc123", "ab 22/14", etc.

Unlike C and C++, string handling can be easily done in java. Java provides a lot of inbuilt functions which make string operations very convenient.

> **Note:**
>
> **A string is always enclosed within double quotes while a character is enclosed in single quotes.**
>
> **Eg: 'a' is a character but "a" is a string. Both are different and have different significance.**

9.2 DECLARATION AND INITIALIZATION OF A STRING

A String can be simply declared as we declare variables.

Eg: String text;

This will create a string with the name 'text'.

Now the initialization is also the same as variables.

Eg: String text="Java";

This will create a string with the name 'text' and "Java" will be stored in it.

9.3 USING IN-BUILT STRING FUNCTIONS

The String class provides us with a variety of pre-defined methods that can be used to perform various operations and manipulations on strings.
To know more about them, consider two strings,

str1="Java", str2="Programming".

Some of the most frequently used methods are discussed below:

(i) charAt(int)
This method returns the character at the given index.

Eg: str1.charAt(3);

This function will return 'a', since 'a' in present at the 4th index of str1.

Eg: str2.charAt(3);

This function will return 'g', since 'g' is present at the 4th index of str2.

(ii) indexOf(char)
This method returns the index of the first occurrence of the character in the string.

Eg: str1.indexOf(a);

This function will return the index of the first occurrence of 'a' in str1 i.e. 1.

Eg: str2.indexOf(a);

This function will return the index of the first occurrence of 'a' in str2 i.e. 5.

(iii) lastindexof(char)
This method returns the index of the last occurrence of the character in the string.

Eg: str1.lastindexOf(g);

It will return 10 since the index of the last occurrence of 'g' in str2 is 10.

(iv) length()
This method computes the length of the string i.e. the total number of characters in the string.

Eg: str1.length();

It will return the value 4.

(v) trim()
This method is used to remove all the blank spaces from the string.

Eg: str="God is great";
    str.trim();

After calling this function,

str="Godisgreat", i.e. the white spaces will be removed.

(vi) substring

This function is used to extract a part of the string.

Eg: str="java is wonderful"

String str1 =str.substring(2,6);

So the string str1 will be "va i".

(vii) compareTo()
The function is used to compare to strings. The syntax is:

string1.compareTo(string2)

The function returns a positive value if string1>string2
It returns a negative value if string1<string2
It returns 0 if both are equal

(viii) equals()
This function is also used to compare two strings. However the syntax is a bit different from the above function. The syntax is:

string1.equals(string2)

The function returns true string1 is equal to string2 otherwise it returns false.

(ix) toUpperCase

This function converts the string to uppercase.

Eg: String s1="java";
   String s2=s1.toUpperCase;

Now s2="JAVA".

(x) toLowerCase

This function converts the string to lowercase.

Eg: String s1="JAVA";
   String s2=s1.toLowerCase;

Now s2="java".

PROGRAMMING EXAMPLES

Ques.9.1 Write a program to enter a string from the user and then display it.

```java
import java.io.*;
public class Print
{
        public static void main(String args[])throws
        IOException
        {
                String str;
                BufferedReader br=new BufferedReader
                (new InputStreamReader(System.in));
                System.out.println("Enter a String");
                str=br.readLine();
                System.out.println("The String you entered is"+str);
        }
}
```

```
str="Hello";
The String you entered is: Hello
```

Ques.9.2 Write a program to enter a string and print its length.

```java
import java.io.*;
public class Print
{
        public static void main(String args[])throws
         IOException
        {
                String str;
                BufferedReader br=new BufferedReader
                (new InputStreamReader(System.in));
                System.out.println("Enter a String");
                str=br.readLine();
                int len=str.length();
                System.out.println("The length is: "+len);
        }
}
```

```
str="java";
The length is: 4
```

Practice Question

Ques.9.3 Write a program to input a string from the user and then display it in reverse order.

Ques.9.4 Write a program to input a string and count the number of vowels and consonants in it.

```
import java.util.*;
public class Count
{
        public static void main(String args[])
        {
                String str;
                char ch;
                int cons=0,vow=0;
                Scanner sc=new Scanner(System.in);
                System.out.println("Enter a String");
                str=sc.nextLine();
                int len=str.length();
                for(int i=0;i<len;i++)
                {
                        ch=str.charAt(i);
                        if(ch=='a'||ch=='e'||ch=='i'||ch=='o'||ch=='u')
                                vow++;
                        else
                                cons++;
                }
                System.out.println("The number of consonants are: "+cons);
                System.out.println("The number of vowels are:"+vow);
        }
}
```

Practice Question

Ques.9.5 Write a program to enter a string and count the occurrence of each vowel.

Ques.9.6 **Write a program to input a string and print the frequency of each character.**

```java
import java.io.*;
public class Frequency
{
        public static void main(String args[])throws
        IOException
        {
                BufferedReader br=new BufferedReader(new
                InputStreamReader(System.in));
                String str;
                char ch;
                int f;
                System.out.println("Enter a String");
                str=br.readLine();
                for(char c='a';c<='z';c++)
                {
                        f=0;
                        for(int i=0;i<str.length();i++)
                        {
                                ch=str.charAt(i);
                                if(ch==c)
                                f++;
                        }
                        if(f!=0)
                                System.out.println("The frequency of "+c+" is
                                "+f);

                }
        }
}
```

```
str="hello";
The frequency of h is:1
The frequency of e is:1
The frequency of l is:2
The frequency of o is:1
```

Ques.9.7 Write a program to enter a word and sort it in alphabetical order.

```java
import java.io.*;
public class WordSort
{
        public static void main(String args[])throws
        IOException
        {
                BufferedReader br=new BufferedReader(new
                InputStreamReader(System.in));
                String str, str1="";
                char ch;
                System.out.println("Enter a String");
                str=br.readLine();
                for(char c='a';c<='z';c++)
                {
                        for(int i=0;i<str.length();i++)
                        {
                                ch=str.charAt(i);
                                if(ch==c)
                                str1+=c;
                        }
                }
                System.out.println("The sorted word is: "+str1);
        }}
```

```
str="programming";
The sorted word is:
aggimmnopr
```

Ques.9.8 Write a program to enter a string in lower case and convert it into upper case without using any in-built function.

```java
import java.util.*;
public class LowertoUpper
{
        public static void main(String args[])
        {
                String str, str1="";
                Scanner sc=new Scanner(System.in);
                System.out.println("Enter a String");
                str=sc.nextLine();
                for(int i=0;i<str.length();i++)
                {
                        char ch=str.charAt(i);
                        str1=str1+(char)(ch-32);
                }
                System.out.println("The String in upper case is:"+str1);
        }
}
```

Practice Question

Ques 9.9 Write a program to enter two strings and print which is greater.

Ques.9.10 Write a program to input a string and check if it is a palindrome.

```java
import java.io.*;
public class Palindrome
{
        public static void main(String args[])throws
        IOException
        {
                String str, rev="";
                char ch;
                BufferedReader br=new BufferedReader(new
                InputStreamReader(System.in));
                System.out.println("Enter a String");
                str=br.readLine();
                int len=str.length();
                for(int i=0;i<len;i++)
                {
                        ch=str.charAt(i);
                        rev=ch+rev;
                }
                if(str.equals(rev))
                        System.out.println("It is a Palindrome");
                else
                        System.out.println("It is not a Palindrome");

        }
}
```

Practice Question

Ques.9.11 Write a program to input a string and insert a character at a particular position.

Ques.9.12 Write a program to enter a string and count the number of alphabets, digits and special characters in it.

```java
import java.util.*;
public class Count
{
        public static void main(String args[])
        {
                String str;
                char ch;
                int alph=0,dig=0,spcl=0;
                Scanner sc=new Scanner(System.in);
                System.out.println("Enter a String");
                str=sc.nextLine();
                for(int i=0;i<str.length();i++)
                {
                        ch=str.charAt(i);
                        if(ch>='a' && ch<='z' || ch>='A' && ch<='Z')
                                alph++;
                        else if(ch>='0' && ch<='9')
                                dig++;
                        else
                                spcl++;
                }
                System.out.println("The number of alphabets are:"+alph);
                System.out.println("The number of digits are:"+dig);
                System.out.println("The number of special
                characters are: "+spcl);
        }
}
```

Ques.9.13 Write a program to enter a string and print each word in a separate line.

```java
import java.io.*;
public class Word
{
    public static void main(String args[])throws IOException
    {
        String str, wrd="";
        char ch;
        BufferedReader br=new BufferedReader(new
        InputStreamReader(System.in));
        System.out.println("Enter a String");
        str=br.readLine();
        str=str+" ";
        for(int i=0;i<str.length();i++)
        {
            ch=str.charAt(i);
            if(ch!=' ')
                wrd=wrd+ch;
            else
            {
                System.out.println(wrd);
                wrd="";
            }
        }
    }
}
```

Ques.9.14 **Write a program to enter a string and print the number of words in it.**

```java
import java.io.*;
public class WordCount
{
        public static void main(String args[])throws
        IOException
        {
                String str;
                char ch;
                int c=0;
                BufferedReader br=new BufferedReader(new
                InputStreamReader(System.in));
                System.out.println("Enter a String");
                str=br.readLine();
                str=str+" ";
                for(int i=0;i<str.length();i++)
                {
                        ch=str.charAt(i);
                        if(ch==' ')
                        c++;
                }
                System.out.println("The total number of words
                are: "+c);
        }
}
```

```
str="God is great";
The total number of words are: 3
```

Ques.9.15 Write a program to enter a string and count the occurrences of the word "the".

```java
import java.util.*;
public class WordFrequency
{
        public static void main(String args[])
        {
                Scanner sc=new Scanner(System.in);
                String str, wrd="";
                int c=0;
                System.out.println("Enter a String");
                str=sc.nextLine();
                str=str+" ";
                for(int i=0;i<str.length();i++)
                {
                        if(str.charAt(i)!= ' ')
                                wrd+=str.charAt(i);
                        else
                        {
                                if(wrd.equals("the"))
                                        c++;
                                wrd="";
                        }
                }
                System.out.println("The frequency of 'the' is:"+c);
        }
}
```

Practice Question

Ques.9.16 Write a program to input a string and delete the occurrences of the word "the".

Ques.9.17 Write a program to delete all the spaces in a sentence without using trim() function.

```
import java.util.*;
class removespace
{
        public static void main (String [] args)
        {
                Scanner st = new Scanner (System.in);
                System.out.println("Enter a sentence");
                String str = st.nextLine();
                String s ="";
                char ch;
                for (int x =0;x<str.length() ;x++)
                {
                        ch = str.charAt(x);
                        if (ch != ' ')
                        {
                                s = s+ch;
                        }
                }
                System.out.println("the sentence without spaces is - "+s);
        }
}
```

Ques.9.18 **Write a program to replace all the occurrences of the character 'a' with 'e'.**

```java
import java.util.*;
class replace
{
        public static void main (String [] args)
        {
                Scanner st = new Scanner (System.in);
                System.out.println("enter a sentence");
                String str = st.nextLine();
                String s="";
                char ch;
                str = str.toLowerCase();
                for (int x =0;x<str.length() ;x++ )
                {
                        ch = str.charAt(x);
                        if (ch == 'e')
                        {
                                s = s+'a';
                        }
                        else
                        {
                                s = s+ch;
                        }
                }
                System.out.println("Sentence after replacing e with a is - "+s);
        }
}
```

```
s="aqua"
Sentence after replacing is: eque
```

Ques.9.19 Write a program to enter a sentence and make every the first letter of every word in upper case.

```java
import java.util.*;
class firstcapital
{
        public static void main (String [] args)
        {
                Scanner st = new Scanner (System.in);
                System.out.println("enter a sentence");
                String str = st.nextLine();
                String s="";
                char ch;
                str = ' '+str;
                for (int x =0;x<str.length() ;x++ )
                {
                        ch = str.charAt(x);
                        if (ch == ' ')
                        {
                                ch = str.charAt(x+1);
                                ch = ch.toUpperCase();
                                s = s+' '+ch;
                                x++;
                        }
                        else
                        {
                                s=s+ch;
                        }
                }
                System.out.println("The string after change is = "+s);
        }
}
```

s="have faith in god"   The new String is: Have Faith In God

Ques.9.20 Write a program to enter a name and print its initials.

```java
import java.util.*;
class initialname
{
        public static void main(String[]args)

        {
                Scanner st = new Scanner (System.in);
                System.out.println("Enter a name");
                String str = st.nextLine();
                String s="";
                char ch;
                int w=0;
                int l = str.length; l--;
                str = ' ' + str;
                while (w==0)
                {
                        ch = str.charAt(l);
                        if (ch != ' ')
                        {
                                s = ch + s;
                        }
                        else
                        {
                                w++;
                                l--;
                        }
                }
                for (int x =l;x>0;x-- )
                {
                        ch = str.charAt(x);
                        if (ch==' ')
                        {
                                s = str.charAt(x+1)+'.'+s;
                        }
                }
                System.out.println("Initials are = "+s);
        }
}
```

CHAPTER -10

SEARCHING SORTING

- Linear Search
- Binary Search
- Bubble Sort
- Selection Sort
- Insertion Sort

10.1 INTRODUCTION

Searching and Sorting techniques are used in a variety of applications where there is a need to search a value in the data or sort the data in ascending or descending order. Eg: In a class record if there is a need to sort the students according to the marks obtained then we use sorting and if we need to search the record of a particular student then we need searching.

Java provides us with two searching techniques:

(i) Linear Search
(ii) Binary Search

Besides searching, the sorting techniques covered in this section are:

(i) Bubble Sort
(ii) Exchange Selection Sort
(iii) Insertion Sort
(iv) Quick Sort
(v) Merge Sort

Let us take them one by one. Programs have been given along with proper explanations of the techniques for clear understanding.

10.2 LINEAR SEARCH

Linear Search is a searching technique in which each of the elements is compared with the search item sequentially one by one. If a match is found then the search is successful and if it is not found then its unsuccessful.

Ques.10.1 Write a program to implement linear search.

```java
import java.io.*;
public class Linear
{
        int arr[]=new int[10];
        int n;
        public void getData()throws IOException
```

```
{
        BufferedReader br=new BufferedReader
        (new InputStreamReader(System.in));
        System.out.println("Enter the elements of the array");
        for(int i=0;i<10;i++)
        {
                arr[i]=Integer.parseInt(br.readLine());
        }
        System.out.println("Enter a value to search");
        n=Integer.parseInt(br.readLine());
}
public void search()
{
        int flag=0,i;
        for(i=0;i<10;i++)
        {
                if(arr[i]==n)
                {
                        flag=1;
                        break;
                }
        }
        if(flag==1)
                System.out.println("Value found at position"+(i+1));
        else
                System.out.println("Value not found");
}
public static void main(String args[])throws IOException
{
        Linear obj=new Linear();
        obj.getData();
        obj.search();
}
}
```

Note:

Consider the following example,

Let the array be:

12	34	11	56	99	123	6	89	21	5

Let the number to be searched be: 56

Now linear search technique proceeds as follows:

1st iteration:

12	34	11	56	99	123	6	89	21	5

↑

12 is not equal to 56 . . . so the next element is compared.

2nd interation:

12	34	11	56	99	123	6	89	21	5

↑

34 is not equal to 56 . . . so the next element is compared.

3rd iteration:

12	34	11	56	99	123	6	89	21	5

↑

11 is not equal to 56 . . . so the next element is compared.

4th iteration:

12	34	11	56	99	123	6	89	21	5

↑

↑ Now the match is found so the program print "value found" and is terminated.

Ques.10.2 Write a program to enter the records of 5 students (Name, Roll and Marks) and print the record of the roll no. entered by the user.

```java
import java.util.*;
public class Student
{
        int r;
        int[] roll={1,2,3,4,5};
        String[] name={" ","Ron","Shivani","Mandeep","Harshit", "Mark"};
        int[] marks={0,78,91,67,87,56};
        public void getData()
        {
                Scanner sc=new Scanner(System.in);
                System.out.println("Enter the roll no. of the student");
                r=sc.nextInt();
        }
        public void search()
        {
                int i;
                for(i=0;i<5;i++)
                {
                        if(roll[i]==r)
                        {
                                break;
                        }
                }
                System.out.println("Roll No. Name \t Marks");
                System.out.println((i+1)+"\t"+name[i+1]+"\t"+marks[i+1]);
        }
        public static void main(String args[])
        {
                Student obj=new Student();
                obj.getData();
                obj.search();
        }
}
```

Practice Question

Ques.10.3 Write a program to initialize an array of 15 elements and search a value entered by user using linear search.

10.3 BINARY SEARCH

Binary search is a technique which uses divide and conquer to search a value. In this method, an array is divided into smaller fragments because of which the number of comparisons become less which makes it a more efficient technique as compared to linear search. But this technique has one major drawback, i.e. before searching an element the array needs to be sorted.

Ques.10.4. Write a program to implement binary search.

```java
import java.util.*;
public class Binary
{
        int arr[]=new int[10];
        int n;
        public void getData()
        {
                Scanner sc=new Scanner(System.in);
                System.out.println("Enter the elements of the array");
                for(int i=0;i<10;i++)
                {
                        arr[i]=sc.nextInt();
                }
                System.out.println("Enter a value to search");
                n=sc.nextInt();
        }
        public void search()
        {
                int beg=0,end=9,mid=0,flag=0;
                while(beg<=end)
        {
        mid=(beg+end)/2;
        if(n==arr[mid])
        {
                flag=1;
                break;
        }
        if(n>arr[mid])
                beg=mid+1;
        if(n<arr[mid])
```

```
        end=mid-1;
}
if(flag==1)
      System.out.println("Value found at position "+(mid+1));
else
      System.out.println("Value not found");
}
public static void main(String args[])
{
      Binary obj=new Binary();
      obj.getData();
      obj.search();
}
}
```

Note:

Consider the same example as above:

Let the array be:

12	32	34	56	99	123	124	150	165	345

Let the number to be searched be 34.

1ˢᵗ iteration:

12	32	34	56	99	123	6	89	21	5

↑

mid=(0+9)/2=4

a[mid] is greater than 34

2ⁿᵈ iteration:

12	32	34	56

↑

mid=(0+3)/2=1

a[mid] is less than 34.

3ʳᵈ iteration:

34	56

↓

mid=(0+1)/2=0

a[mid] is equal to 34

Search successful

Ques.10.6 Write a program to enter 20 numbers in an array and search an element using binary search.

10.4 BUBBLE SORT

Ques.10.7 Write a program to enter an array of 10 elements and sort it using bubble sort.

```
import java.io.*;
public class Bubble
{
    int arr[]=new int[10];
    public void getData()throws IOException
    {
        BufferedReader br=new BufferedReader(new
        InputStreamReader(System.in));
        System.out.println("Enter the elements of the array");
        for(int i=0;i<10;i++)
        {
            arr[i]=Integer.parseInt(br.readLine());
        }
    }
    public void sort()
    {
        int temp;
        for(int i=1;i<10;i++)
        {
            for(int j=0;j<(10-i);j++)
            {
                if(arr[j]>arr[j+1])
                {
                    temp=arr[j];
                    arr[j]=arr[j+1];
                    arr[j+1]=temp;
                }
            }
        }
    }
    public void display()
    {
        System.out.println("The array in sorted order is :");
        for(int i=0;i<10;i++)
```

```
        {
                System.out.print(arr[i]+"\t");
        }
}
public static void main(String args[])throws IOException
{
        Bubble obj=new Bubble();
        obj.getData();
        obj.sort();
        obj.display();
}
}
```

Note: The bubble sort is implemented as follows:
Eg: Consider the following array:

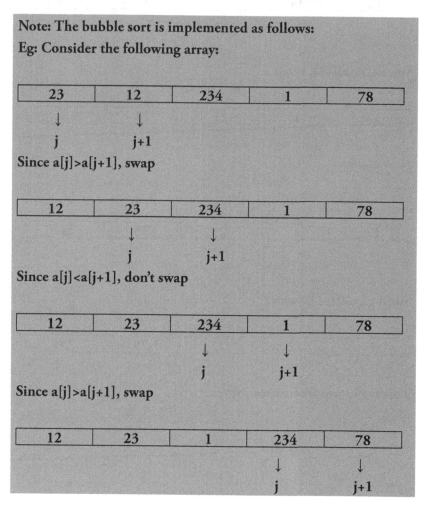

Since a[j]>a[j+1], swap

12	23	1	78	234

    ↓   ↓

    j   j+1

Since a[j]<a[j+1], don't swap

12	23	1	78	234

        ↓   ↓

        j   j+1

Since a[j]>a[j+1], swap

12	1	23	78	234

12	1	23	78	234

    ↓   ↓

    j   j+1

Since a[j]>a[j+1], swap

1	12	23	78	234

This is the required sorted array.

Ques.10.8 Write a program to enter the marks of 10 students and sort them using bubble sort.

```java
import java.io.*;
public class Bubble
{
        int arr[]=new int[10];
        public void getData()throws IOException
        {
                BufferedReader br=new BufferedReader(new
                InputStreamReader(System.in));
                System.out.println("Enter the marks of 10 students");
                for(int i=0;i<10;i++)
                {
                        arr[i]=Integer.parseInt(br.readLine());
                }
        }
        public void sort()
        {
                int temp;
                for(int i=1;i<10;i++)
                {
                        for(int j=0;j<(10-i);j++)
                        {
                                if(arr[j]>arr[j+1])
                                {
                                        temp=arr[j];
                                        arr[j]=arr[j+1];
                                        arr[j+1]=temp;
                                }
                        }
                }
        }
        public void display()
        {
                System.out.println("The marks in sorted order are:");
                for(int i=0;i<10;i++)
                {
                        System.out.print(arr[i]+"\t");
```

```
        }
    }
public static void main(String args[])throws IOException
    {
        Bubble obj=new Bubble();
        obj.getData();
        obj.sort();
        obj.display();
    }
}
```

Practice Question

Ques.10.9 Write a program to enter the heights of 5 students in a class and sort it using bubble sort.

10.5 SELECTION SORT

Ques.10.10 Write a program to implement selection sort.

```
import java.io.*;
public class Selection
{
        int arr[]=new int[10];
        public void getData()throws IOException
        {
                BufferedReader br=new BufferedReader(new
                InputStreamReader(System.in));
                System.out.println("Enter the elements of the array");
                for(int i=0;i<10;i++)
                {
                        arr[i]=Integer.parseInt(br.readLine());
                }
        }
        public void sort()
        {
                int temp;
                for(int i=0;i<10;i++)
                {
                        for(int j=i+1;j<10;j++)
                        {
                                if(arr[i]>arr[j])
                                {
                                        temp=arr[i];
                                        arr[i]=arr[j];
                                        arr[j]=temp;
                                }
                        }
                }
        }
        public void display()
        {
                System.out.println("Array after sorting is");
                for(int i=0;i<10;i++)
                {
```

```java
            System.out.print(arr[i]+"\t");
        }
    }
    public static void main(String args[])throws IOException
    {
        Selection obj=new Selection();
        obj.getData();
        obj.sort();
        obj.display();
    }
}
```

10.6 INSERTION SORT

Ques.10.11 **Write a program to implement insertion sort.**

```java
import java.io.*;
public class Selection
{
    int arr[]=new int[10];
    public void getData()throws IOException
    {
        BufferedReader br=new BufferedReader(new
        InputStreamReader(System.in));
        System.out.println("Enter the elements of the array");
        for(int i=0;i<10;i++)
        {
            arr[i]=Integer.parseInt(br.readLine());
        }
    }
    public void sort()
    {
        int temp;
        for(int i=0;i<10;i++)
        {
            for(int j=i+1;j<10;j++)
            {
                if(arr[i]>arr[j])
```

```
                {
                        temp=arr[i];
                        arr[i]=arr[j];
                        arr[j]=temp;
                }
        }
    }
}
public void display()
{
        System.out.println("Array after sorting is");
        for(int i=0;i<10;i++)
        {
                System.out.print(arr[i]+"\t");
        }
}
public static void main(String args[])throws IOException
{
        Selection obj=new Selection();
        obj.getData();
        obj.sort();
        obj.display();
}
}
```

Practice Question

Ques.10.12 Write a program to enter an array of 10 elements, sort it using insertion sort and them search a value using bubble sort.

CHAPTER 11

INHERITANCE

- Concept of Inheritance
- Use of extends
- Types of inheritance
- Access specifiers
- Short-answer questions

11.1 CONCEPT OF INHERITANCE

In simple words, inheritance is the phenomenon by which one class can acquire the properties of another class. The class which derives the properties of another class is called the derived class and the class which is being derived is called the base class. The derived class contains not only the methods and the attributes of the base class but it also has its own methods and attributes. In other words we can say that it adds to the functionality of the base class.

Eg:

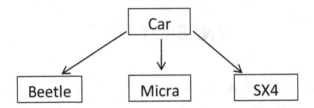

In the above example 'Car' is the base or the parent class, while 'Beetle, Micra, SX4' are the derived or child classes. Now although all the derived classes are examples of cars but still every class is different from the other. The cars may vary like different manufacturer or mileage or engine power, etc. But they have things in common like they have four wheels, four doors, etc.

1.2 TYPES OF INHERITANCE

A subclass may be inherited in various ways in java. There are mainly five types of inheritance in java.

(i) Single Inheritance

In this type of inheritance a sub class is derived from a single super class. The derived class has the functionality of the base class as well as its own functionality. However the base class has no control over the data members and member functions of the derived class.

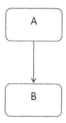

Over here class 'A' is termed as the base class and class 'B' is termed as derived class.

(ii) Multi-level Inheritance

In multi-level Inheritance, a new class is derived from a class, which is in-turn derived from another base class.

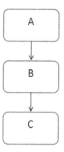

In the above diagram class C is derived from class B which is in-turn derived from class A. So, Class A acts as base class for class B and class B acts as base class for class C.

(iii) Multiple Inheritance

In this type of inheritance, a single class is derived from a number of base classes.

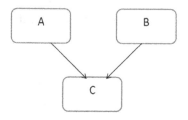

Over here class A and class B act as base classes for class C. However is java we cannot implement multiple inheritance directly. It can be done through **interface.**

(iv) Hierarchical Inheritance

In this type of inheritance multiple classes inherit from a single base class.

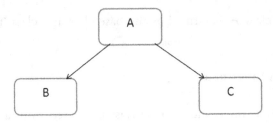

As it is quite clear class B and class C both inherit from a single base class A.

(v) Hybrid Inheritance

Hybrid inheritance is nothing but a collection of two or more inheritance.

Eg:

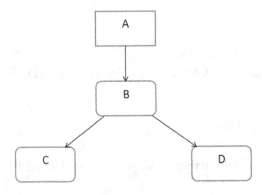

The above example implements both single inheritance and hierarchical inheritance.

PROGRAMMING EXAMPLES

Ques.11.1 Write a program that implement single inheritance.

```
class Display
{
     public void show()
     {
          System.out.println("Hello");
     }
}
public class Display1 extends Display
{
     public void show1()
     {
          System.out.println("World");
     }
     public static void main(String args[])
     {
          Display1 obj=new Display1();
          obj.show();
          obj.show1();
     }
}
```

Program Analysis:

In the above program, although the method show() is defined in the base class but still the object of the derived class **obj** is able to access it.

Ques.11.2 Design a class that takes input of two numbers and design another class which prints their values.

```
import java.util.*;
class Parent
{
     int a, b;
     public void getData()
```

```
        {
                Scanner sc=new Scanner(System.in);
                System.out.println("Enter the value of a and b");
                a=sc.nextInt();
                b=sc.nextInt();
        }
}
class Child extends Parent
{
        public void display()
        {
                System.out.println("a= "+a);
                System.out.println("b= "+b);
        }
}
public class Main
{
        public static void main(String args[])
        {
                Child obj=new Child();
                obj.getData();
                obj.display();
        }
}
```

Program Analysis:

The data members **a and b** belong to the **Parent** class but since the **Child** class extends the Parent class so it can access the data members of its base class.

So, we have seen that a child class object can access the data members and member methods of the base class.

But, in some cases they remain inaccessible to the derived class. Before, going into them let's take up the **access specifiers.**

Ques.11.3 **Write a program to demonstrate the use of private.**

```java
import java.util.*;
class Parent
{
        private int a;
        public void getData()
        {
                Scanner sc=new Scanner(System.in);
                System.out.println("Enter the value of a ");
                a=sc.nextInt();
        }
}
class Child extends Parent
{
        public void display()
        {
                int b=a;
                System.out.println("The value of b is: "+b);
        }
}
public class Main
{
        public static void main(String args[])
        {
                Child obj=new Child();
                obj.getData();
                obj.display();
        }
}
```

Program Analysis:

The above programming is doing a very simple task. It is assigning the value of **a** in the base class to **b** in the derived class. But the compiler will report an error, since a has a private access so it is not accessible to the object of the derived class.

Ques.11.4 Write a program to access a private data member indirectly.

```java
import java.util.*;
class Parent
{
        private int a;
        public void getData()
        {
                Scanner sc=new Scanner(System.in);
                System.out.println("Enter the value of a ");
                a=sc.nextInt();
        }
}
class Child extends Parent
{
        public void display()
        {
                int b=a;
                System.out.println("The value of b is: "+b);
        }
}
public class Main
{
        public static void main(String args[])
        {
                Child obj=new Child();
                obj.getData();
                obj.display();
        }
}
```

Program Analysis:

In this program also we are doing the same task as above. But notice that we are not directly using **a** in the derived class. Instead, we have a function **geta()** which returns the value of **a** which is then being used in the derived class.

Ques.11.5 **Write a program to show multi-level inheritance.**

```java
import java.util.*;
class GrandParent
{
        int a;
        public void geta()
        {
                Scanner sc=new Scanner(System.in);
                System.out.println("Enter the value of a ");
                a=sc.nextInt();
        }
}
class Parent extends GrandParent
{
        int b;
        public void getb()
        {
                Scanner sc=new Scanner(System.in);
                System.out.println("Enter the value of b ");
                b=sc.nextInt();
        }
}
class Child extends Parent
{
        int sum;
        public void display()
        {
                sum=a+b;
                System.out.println("The sum is: "+sum);
        }
}
public class Main
{
        public static void main(String args[])
        {
                Child obj=new Child();
                obj.geta();
                obj.getb();
```

```
        obj.display();
    }
}
```

Program Analysis:

In the above program **a** is a data member of the GrandParent class, **b** is the data member of Parent class(which extends GrandParent) and **sum** is the data member of the Child class(which extends Parent). The Child class object accesses the values of a and b and calculates the sum.

CHAPTER 12

POLYMORPHISM

- Meaning of polymorphism
- Types of polymorphism
- Function overloading
- Function overriding
- Use of super keyword in java

12.1 POLYMORPHISM

Before getting into the practical details for understanding polymorphism, let's consider a scenario. Eg: When you are in school, your behavior is different with respect to your classmates and teachers. You behave in a disciplined and well-mannered way. But when you come home you are more comfortable and behave in a normal, free and casual manner. Although you are one and same person only but still your behavior is different according to the changing circumstances.

In the same way polymorphism is used in java. Polymorphism is nothing but the existence in more than one form or we can also say that **polymorphism is the ability of an object to take more than one form.**

12.2 IMPLEMENTING POLYMORPHISM

In Java, polymorphism is implemented in two ways:

    (i) Function Overloading
    (ii) Function Overriding

12.3 FUNCTION OVERLOADING

Function Overloading is a phenomenon in which a single class contains multiple functions which have the same function name but differ in the number or the type of parameters or we can say that they **differ in the function signature.**

Eg:
```
class A
{
        public int xyz(int a)
        {
                // set of statements
        }
        public int xyz(int a, int b)
        {
                //set of statements
```

```
        }
}
```

In the above piece of code, although the function name is the same but it has different number of parameters. The first function has 1 parameter while the second has 2. So every time a call is made to the above functions, the functions gets called depending upon the number of arguments passed in the calling statement.

Ques.12.1 **Write a program to perform addition of two and three numbers using polymorphism.**

```
import java.io.*;
public class Addition
{
      public void sum(int a, int b)
      {
            int c=a+b;
            System.out.println("The sum is: "+c);
      }
      public void sum(int a, int b, int c)
      {
            int d=a+b+c;
            System.out.println("The sum is: "+d);
      }
      public static void main(String args[])
      {
            Addition obj=new Addition();
            obj.sum(2,3);
            obj.sum(4,5,6);
      }
}
```

Program Analysis:

In the above program when a call is made to **sum(2,3)** then the first function gets executed since it has got two arguments while when a call is made to **sum(4,5,6)** then the second function is executed since it has three arguments. So, it is quite clear that only that functions is called which has the same number or type of parameters when the call is being made.

Ques.12.2 **Write a program to find the area of a circle, rectangle and square.**

```java
import java.io.*;
public class Area
{
        public void area(double r)
        {
                double a=3.14*r*r;
                System.out.println("The area is: "+a);
        }
        public void area(double l, double b)
        {
                double a=l*b;
                System.out.println("The area is: "+a);
        }
        public void area(int s)
        {
                int a=s*s;
                System.out.println("The area is: "+a);
        }
        public static void main(String args[])throws
        IOException
        {
                Area obj=new Area();
                BufferedReader br=new BufferedReader(new
                InputStreamReader(System.in));
                System.out.println("Press 1 to find the area of
                circle");
                System.out.println("Press 2 to find the area of
                rectangle");
                System.out.println("Press 3 to find the area of
                square");
                int ch=Integer.parseInt(br.readLine());
                switch(ch)
                {
```

```
case 1:
        System.out.println("Enter the radius of the
        circle");
        double r=Double.parseDouble(br.readLine());
        obj.area(r);
        break;
case 2:
        System.out.println("Enter the length and
        breadth");
        double l=Double.parseDouble(br.readLine());
        double b=Double.parseDouble(br.readLine());
        obj.area(l, b);
        break;
    case 3:
        System.out.println("Enter the length of side
        of square");
        int s=Integer.parseInt(br.readLine());
        obj.area(s);
        break;
        }
    }
}
```

Program Analysis:

In the above program, firstly the user will be prompted to choose the shape for which he wants to find the area for.

Then, the user will be asked to provide the values according to the geometrical figure chosen. Eg: If it's a circle, then the user has to enter radius, if it's a rectangle then the user has to enter length and breadth, etc.

Now the call is being made to the function according to the choice of the user. When one argument i.e. radius is passed to the function area() then, it will find the area of circle but when two arguments i.e. length and breadth are passed to the function area() then the area of rectangle is calculated.

Practice Question

Ques.12.3 Write a program to implement function overloading.

12.4 FUNCTION OVERRIDING

In simple words we can say that overriding is a feature in java in methods in the inherited classes can have the same name as that of methods of the base class.

However technically, function overriding is a feature in which a sub class or a child class can provide a specific implementation of a function that is already present in the base class. To understand this phenomenon let us understand a simple example.

```
class abc
{
      void display()
      {
            System.out.println("In Parent Class");
      }
}
class xyz extends abc
{
      void display()
      {
            System.out.println("In Child Class");
      }
}
public class Main
{
      public static void main(String args[])
      {
            abc obj1=new abc();
            abc obj2=new xyz();
            obj1.display();
            obj2.display();
      }
}
```

In the above example, although obj2 has abc reference but it is a xyz object. Therefore in the runtime, the method in the child class gets executed.

Let's take another example,

```
class abc
{
        void display()
        {
                System.out.println("In Parent Class");
        }
}
class xyz extends abc
{
        void display()
        {
                System.out.println("In Child Class");
        }
        void show()
        {
          System.out.println("Hello");
        }
}

public class Main
{
        public static void main(String args[])
        {
                abc obj1=new abc():
                abc obj2=new xyz();
                obj1.display();
                obj2.display();
                obj2.show();
        }
}
```

In this example,
obj2.show() will return an error since obj2 has the reference of the class abc and abc has no method named show.

The use of super keyword

The super keyword is used to invoke the superclass version of a method. Let's see an example first,

```
class abc
{
        void display()
        {
                System.out.println("In Parent Class");
        }
}
class xyz extends abc
{
        void display()
        {
                super.display();
                System.out.println("In Child Class");
        }
}
public class Main
{
        public static void main(String args[])
        {
                abc obj=new xyz();
                obj.display();
        }
}
```

The output of the above program is:
In Parent Class
In Child Class

If you notice, super.display() is written in the method of the base class. So, when the child class method is invoked, firstly the control is transferred to the base class method and then the child class method is executed.

Just as is the case with methods, same is the case with data members. If we want to use a data member of the base class which has been overridden in the derived class then we use the super keyword.

Eg:

```
class abc
{
        int a=10;
}
class xyz extends abc
{
        int a=20;
        void display()
        {
                System.out.println("The value of a in sub class is: "+a);
                System.out.println("The value of a in base class is: "+super.a);
        }
}
public class Main
{
        public static void main(String args[])
        {
                xyz obj=new xyz();
                obj.display();
        }
}
```

The output of the above program is:
The value of a in sub class is 20
The value of a in base class is 10

This is because of the fact that we have used **super.a** in the second printing statement which invokes the base class version of a.

Practice Question

Ques.12.4 Write a program that demonstrates function overriding.

7.7 CONSTRUCTOR OVERLOADING

As in the case with functions, a constructor can also be overloaded. We can create any number of constructors in a class as per our need. To understand this concept, examine the code below:

```
public class Hello
{
    String a;
    Hello()
    {
    System.out.println("In default Constructor");
    }
    Hello(String name)
    {
        a=name;
    System.out.println("Hello "+a);
    System.out.println("In paramterized constructor");
    public static void main(String args[])
    {
        Hello obj1=new Hello();
        Hello obj2=new Hello("Robert");
    }
}
```

The output of the above code will be:
In default constructor
Hello Robert
In parameterized constructor

So, it is quite clear that here we have two constructors with the same name but different **signature.**

7.8 CONSTRUCTOR CHAINING

Consider a scenario where a child class inherits a parent class. Now when an object of the child class is created its constructor is invoked. However, to invoke the constructor of the base class we use the **super** keyword to pass the argument to the parent class constructor.

Observe the code below:

```
class Parent
{
        int x;
        Parent(int a)
        {
                x=a;
        }
}
class Child
{
        int y;
        Child(int a, int b)
        {
                super(a);
                y=b;
        }
        System.out.println("Value of x is: "+x);
        System.out.println("Value of y is: "+y);
}
```

12.5 QUESTION HOUR

(i)   What do you understand by polymorphism?
(ii) Explain the concept of function overloading.
(iii) What is the difference between function signature and function prototype?
(iv) Write a program that explains polymorphism.
(v)   Explain function overriding.
(vi) What is the difference between function overloading and overriding?
(vii) What is the use of super keywords?

CHAPTER 13

EXCEPTION HANDLING

- What are exceptions?
- Error and Exception
- Exception handling
- try{} and catch{}
- throws clause
- Importance of Exception Handling

Programs at a glance

➢ Program that generates an exception.
➢ Program to handle the above exception.
➢ Program to make use of the finally clause in the above program.
➢ Program to generate ArrayIndexOufOfBound exception and then handle it.
➢ Program that throws an exception to the calling method.
➢ Program to catch an InputOutput Exception using throws clause.

13.1 INTRODUCTION

You might have observed that not every time your program gets compiled and executed successfully. Sometimes an error occurs during compilation while sometimes it occurs during the execution of the program.

So we can say that an error is anything that hampers or stops the normal execution of the program. Broadly errors are mainly of two types:

(i) Compile-time Errors

These are general syntactical errors that are reported during the compilation of the program. They occur usually due to the violation of the syntax.

Eg: int x
It will report an error since the ; is missing.
Let's take another example,
System.out.println("Hi");
It will report an error since 's' should be in capitals.

It is generally easier to identify and rectify syntactical errors.

(ii) Run-time Errors

These are the errors which are reported during the execution of the program. They usually occur when an exception is raised. An **exception** is an unexpected situation that may arise during the execution of the program.

Eg: a=10/0;

This will result in an exception since division by 0 is not defined.

Let's see another exception generating example,

Consider the following array 'arr':

4	3	67	7	90

In the following array if we refer to, arr[5] then it will result in an exception since we are accessing the array index beyond the size of the array.

As compared to compile-time errors it is sometimes difficult to identify and manage exception generating code. Because of this reason Java has provided with the tools of exception handling. **Exception Handling** involves the various means to handle such unexpected situations during the execution of the program.

Java provides us with two major exception handling tools. They are:

(i) try-catch

(ii) throws

13.2 try{ } and catch { }

In this way of exception handling, we place the code in which the exception may arise in the try block and the statements required to deal with the exception in catch block.

A java program may include multiple catch blocks where each block can be made capable of handling a particular type of exception.

The syntax is expressed below:

```
try
{
        //exception generating code
}
catch(Exception e)
{
        //exception handling code
}
```

Java also provides us with the **finally** block. This includes the piece of code that is always executed regardless of the fact that whether an exception is generated or not.

The syntax using the finally block is as follows:

```
try
{
        //exception generating code
}
catch(Exception e)
{
        //exception handling code
}
finally
{
        //statements which are always exceuted
}
```

Note: A try block must be accompanied by a catch or finally block. It can have multiple catch blocks but only one finally block.

13.3 The use of throws

You would have noticed that in the programs before we have written the 'throws' clause after some of the methods, well now is the time to know the reason of it.

Whenever we want to pass an exception out of a method then we use the **'throws clause'**.

Eg:
public static void main(String args[])throws IOException

This means that when an exception will occur in this method then it will automatically be handled by the exception handler.

13.4 IMPORTANCE OF EXCEPTION HANDLING

Exception Handling forms an important part of programming when its done on serious basis. The advantages are as follows:

(i) It separates the normal code from the exception generating code. So when an exception occurs we know that which part is responsible for it. We don't have to search the entire program for it.

(ii) When an exception occurs, exception handling allows the program to execute and deal with the exception in an appropriate manner.

PROGRAMMING EXAMPLES

Ques.13.1 Write a program that generates an exception.

```
public class Divide
{
        static public void div()
        {
                int a=2,b=0;
                float c=a/b;
                System.out.println(c);
        }
        public static void main(String args[])
        {
                div();
        }
}
```

The exception generated is:

```
java.lang.ArithmeticException: / by zero
        at Divide.div(Divide.java:6)
        at Divide.main(Divide.java:11)
```

Ques.13.2 **Write a program to handle the above exception.**

```java
public class Divide
{
        static public void div()
        {
                int a=2,b=0;
                try
                {
                        float c=a/b;
                        System.out.println(c);
                }
                catch(Exception e)
                {
                        System.out.println("Exception generated:"
                        +e.getMessage());
                }
        }
        public static void main(String args[])
        {
                div();
        }
}
```

The output is:

Exception generated: / by zero

Ques.13.3 Write a program to make use of the finally clause in the above program.

```java
import java.util.*;
public class Divide
{
        static public void div()
        {
                Scanner sc=new Scanner(System.in);
                int a, b;
                System.out.println("Enter the values of a and b");
                a=sc.nextInt();
                b=sc.nextInt();
                float c=-1;
                try
                {
                        c=a/b;
                        System.out.println(c);
                }
                catch(Exception e)
                {
                        System.out.println("Exception generated:"
                        +e.getMessage());
                }
                finally
                {
                        System.out.println("The quotient is: "+c);
                }

        }
        public static void main(String args[])
        {
                div();
        }
}
```

When the value of b is 0, the output is:

Exception generated: / by zero
The quotient is: -1.0

Practice Question

Ques.13.4 Write a program to generate ArrayIndexOufOfBound exception and then handle it.

Ques.13.5 Write a program that throws an exception to the calling method.

```
import java.io.*;
public class Number
{
        public void getInput()throws IOException
        {
        BufferedReader br=new BufferedReader(new
        InputStreamReader(System.in));
        int n=Integer.parseInt(br.readLine());
        public static void main(String args[])throws
        IOException
        {
                Number obj=new Number();
                obj.getInput();
        }
}
```

When an exception will occur in this method then it will automatically be handled by the exception handler.

Ques.13.5 Write a program to catch an InputOutput Exception using throws clause.

13.5 QUESTION HOUR

(i)   What is an error?
(ii)   What is the difference between compile-time and run-time error?
(iii) What do you mean by exception?
(iv)   What is the difference between error and exception?
(v)   Explain the use of try{} and catch{} with the help of an example.
(vi)   How throws clause enables exception handling?
(vii) List the various benefits of exception handling.
(viii) What is the difference between throw and throws.

CHAPTER 14

STACKS AND QUEUES

- Concept of Data Structures
- Introduction to Stacks
- Operations on Stacks
- Introduction to Queues
- Operations on Queues

Programs at a Glance

Stack

- Program to insert an element into a stack.
- Program to delete an element from the top of the stack.
- Program to implement push and pop operations in a stack. (The data members should be initialized with legal initial values)
- Program to convert an infix expression to a postfix expression.
- Program to convert an infix expression to a prefix expression.

Queue

- Program to push an element in a queue.
- Program to pop an element from a queue.
- Program to implement push and pop operations in a queue. (The data members should be initialized with legal initial values)
- Program to insert an element in a circular queue.
- Program to delete an element from a circular queue.

14.1 INTRODUCTION

You have already been introduced to single and double dimensional arrays in previous chapters. We know that an array is nothing but a collection of elements which enables efficient storage and management of data. However, if we take the bigger aspect, sometimes the data is too large for an array to handle. An array basically has the following disadvantages:

(i) The size of the array should be known at the time of declaration of the array.
(ii) The size of the array cannot be changed once it is declared.
(iii) Basic operation like searching or sorting may take time when handling large amount of data.

To overcome the disadvantages of arrays, we use data structures. Data structure is basically a concept of creating logical structures in the memory by using small space of the primary memory or in simple words we can say that it is a collection of data in a well defined manner. Eg: Stack, Queue, Linked list, etc.

14.2 STACK

A Stack is a linear data structure based upon the LIFO(Last In First Out) principle. According to this, the data that is inserted in the end is the first one to be removed. The two basic operations on a stack involves push and pop. It is similar to an array, but it has a major distinction that the element can be inserted or removed only from the top of the stack.

14.2.1 INSERTION IN A STACK

Inserting an element in a stack Is called push. When we insert an element in a stack, the top increases by 1 and the new element is inserted. To insert a new element the top is again increased by 1.

Consider the following stack,

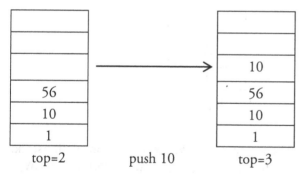

top=2   push 10   top=3

A new element can be inserted till the time the stack is not full. When this happens, the condition is called STACK OVERFLOW.

Note: A stack is said to be full when the top of the stack is equal to one less than the size of the array i.e. top=size-1.

Algorithm to insert an element in a stack

Step 1 - check for overflow.
       if (pointer == size) then display "STACK OVERFLOW".
Step 2 - increase stack pointer
       pointer++.
Step 3 - push the element.
       stack[pointer] = element

14.2.2 DELETION IN A STACK

Since a stack is a LIFO structure, so the deletion takes place from the top of the stack. The element that is inserted in the end is the first one to be removed. When a element is popped, then the stack pointer is decreased by 1.

Eg: Consider the following stack:

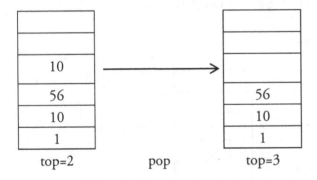

An element is deleted when a value is present at the top of the stack. When the stack is empty, a condition arises called STACK UNDERFLOW.

Note: A stack is said to be empty when it contains no value i.e. the stack pointer is equal to -1.

Algorithm to delete an element from a stack

Step 1- check for underflow
        if (pointer == null) then display "STACK UNDERFLOW".
Step 2 - pop out the value
        value = stack[pointer].
Step 3 - decrement pointer
        pointer--.

14.2.3 PEEP INTO A STACK

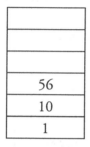

The peek() method will return the element i.e. present at the top of the stack i.e. 56.

14.2.4 SIZE OF THE STACK

The size() method will return the total number of elements in the stack. It is always equal to the value of top+1 i.e. size=3.

Ques.14.1 Write a program to insert an element into a stack.

```java
import java.util.*;
public class Push
{
    public static void main (String[]args)
    {
        Scanner st = new Scanner (System.in);
        int stack[] = new int [10];
        int size=10, n, p;
        int p = -1;
        System.out.println("Enter the element to be pushed");
        n = st.nextInt();
        for (int x=1; x<10; x++)
        {
        stack[x] = 0;
    }
    if (p == (size-1))
    {
        System.out.println("STACK OVERFLOW");
    }
    else
    {
        p++;
        stack[p] = n;
    }
}}
```

Ques.14.2 Write a program to delete an element from the top of the stack.

```java
import java.util.*;
public class Pop
{
        public static void main (String[]args)
        {
                Scanner st = new Scanner (System.in);
                int stack[] = new int [10];
                int size=10, n, p;
                int p = -1;
                for (int x=1; x<10; x++)
                {
                        stack[x] = 0;
                }
                if (p == -1)
                {
                        System.out.println("STACK UNDERFLOW");
                }
                else
                {
                        n = stack[p];
                        System.out.println("Popped element is -"+ n);
                        p--;
                }
        }
}
```

Ques.14.3 Write a program to implement push and pop operations in a stack. (The data members should be initialized with legal initial values)

14.3 NOTATIONS

Notations are basically the various ways by which we can write an algebraic expression. There are three types of notations:

(i) infix notation

This is the normal mathematical style of writing an expression. Eg: A+B. In this form of notation the operator is placed in between the operands. Although this notation is easier to write and understand for the human mind but the computers face difficulties in parsing them. So, the computers use postfix and prefix notations.

(ii) postfix notation

In this notation, the operator is written after the operands. Eg: If the infix expression is A+B then its postfix notation will be AB+. The order of evaluation is always from left to right.

Eg: Consider the following expression,

Infix Notation: (A+B)*(C+D)
Postfix Notation: (AB+)*(CD+)
                      AB+CD+*

Practice Question

Ques.14.4 Write a program to convert an infix expression to a postfix expression.

(iii) prefix notation

In this notation, the operator is written before the operands. Eg: If the infix expression is A+B, then the prefix notation will be +AB. The order of evaluation is from left to right.

Consider the following expression,

Infix Notation : (A+B)*(C+D)

Postfix Notation: (+AB)*(+CD)
$$*+AB+CD$$

Practice Question

Ques.14.5 Write a program to convert an infix expression to a prefix expression.

Ques.14.6 Write a program with the following details:

class name	:	stack
data member	:	
int stk[]	:	array to hold integer elements of maximum 200.
int capacity	:	store maximum capacity of integer array
int top	:	to point the index of topmost element
methods	:	
stack()	:	constructor
stack(int cap)	:	constructor to initialize cap to capacity and -1 to top
void push(int v)	:	push v into stack on the top, if possible else if stack is full display "STACK OVERFLOW"
int pop()	:	removes an element from the top of the stack and return it, if possible else display "STACK UNDERFLOW" if stack is empty.
void print()	:	to display the elements of the stack if possible else display "STACK UNDERFLOW"

Specify the class 'stack' giving details of the constructors and the functions given above. write a menu driven program with options push - 1, pop - 2, show stack - 3, quit - 4, and using switch case invoke the functions depending upon the choice entered.

14.4 QUEUE

Queue is another linear data structure but it is based upon FIFO(First In First Out) principle. According to this principle, the element that is added first is the first one to be removed. It also has two basic operations i.e. push and pop. An element is inserted at the rear end of the queue and it is removed from the front end. This means that the insertion and deletion takes place from two ends.

14.4.1 INSERTION IN A QUEUE

An element is inserted in a queue using the push operation. As discussed above, an element is added at the rear end of the queue.
Consider the following queue,

3	4			

↓ front 0   ↓ rear 1

Now when we insert a value in a queue, i.e. push 10 then,

3	4	10		

↓ front 0   ↓ rear 1

So, it is quite clear that when an element is inserted in a stack the position of the rear is increased by 1. Sometimes, a condition may arise that the queue is full i.e.

3	4	10	12	67

↓ front   ↓ rear

In this case the value of rear is equal to the size-1. So when the push operation is called it display an error messages informing that the queue is full.

Algorithm for insertion in a queue

Step 1: check for overflow
    if (r == (size-1)) then display "QUEUE OVERFLOW".
Step 2: set rear end pointer
    if (f == null && r == null) then set f =0 and r =0.
    else set r++.
Step 3: insertion of element
    queue[r] = item.

14.4.2 DELETION IN A QUEUE

An element is removed from the queue using the pop operation. Since the elements are removed in the same order in which they are added, so the deletion takes place from the front end of the queue.
Consider the following queue,

5	7	10		

  ↓   ↓
front   rear
 0

After executing the pop operation, the queue becomes,

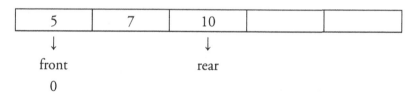

	7	10		

      ↓   ↓
    front rear
     1   2

So, it can be concluded that when an element is removed from the queue, the front is increased by 1.

Sometimes a queue may be empty, i.e.

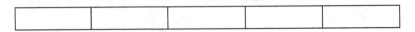

In this case the value of both front and rear is -1. So when the pop operation is called it displays an error messages stating that the queue is empty.

Algorithm for deletion in a queue

Step 1 - check for underflow
   if (f == -1 && r == -1) then display "QUEUE UNDERFLOW".
Step 2 - delete the element
   value = queue[front]
Step 3 - set pointers
   if (f == r) then set f == -1 and r == -1
   else set f++

Ques.14.7 **Write a program to push an element in a queue.**

```java
import java.util.*;
public class Push
{
        public static void main (String[]args)
        {
                Scanner st = new Scanner (System.in);
                int q[] = new int [10];
                int size=10, n, f, r;
                int p = r = -1;
                System.out.println("Enter the element to be inserted");
                n = st.nextInt();
                for (int x=1; x<10; x++)
                {
                        q[x] = 0;
                }
                if (r == (size-1))
                {
                        System.out.println("QUEUE OVERFLOW");
                }
                else
                {
                if (f == -1 && r == -1)
                {
                        f = 0;
                        r = 0;
                }
                else
                {
                        r++;
                }
                q[r] = n;
                }
        }
}
```

Ques.14.8 Write a program to pop an element from a queue.

```java
import java.util.*;
public class Pop
{
        public static void main (String[]args)
        {
                Scanner st = new Scanner (System.in);
                int q[] = new int [10];
                int size=10, n,  ;
                int p = r = -1;
                for (int x=1; x<10; x++)
                {
                        q[x] = 0;
                }
                if (f == -1&& r == -1)
                {
                        System.out.println("QUEUE UNDERFLOW");
                }
                else
                {
                        n = q[f];
                if (f == r)
                {
                        f = -1;
                        r = -1;
                }
                else
                {
                        f++;
                }
                }
        }
}
```

Practice Question

Ques.14.9 Write a program to implement push and pop operations in a queue. (The data members should be initialized with legal initial values)

Ques.14.10 Queue is an entity which can hold elements. The queue follows the principle of FIFO. Define a class as follows:

class name	:	queue
data member	:	
int q[]	:	array to hold the integer elements
int capacity	:	to hold maximum capacity of array.
int f	:	front pointer
int r	:	rear pointer
methods	:	
queue()	:	constructor
queue(int limit)	:	constructor to initialize limit to capacity, -1 to f and r
void push (int n)	:	adds the element to the queue from rear end if possible, else displays "QUEUE OVERFLOW"
int pop()	:	removes and returns one element from the top of the queue if possible, else display "QUEUE UNDERFLOW"
void display( )	:	to display the elements of the queue if possible else display "QUEUE IS EMPTY"

Specify the class queue giving the details of the methods given above. write a menu driven program with options push - 1, pop - 2, show stack - 3, quit - 4, and using switch case invoke the functions depending upon the choice entered.

14.5 CIRCULAR QUEUE

A normal queue has a major disadvantage. Itdoes not allow insertion of element if rear pointer points to the size of the queue even if there are empty spaces available at the front of the queue. This problem is sorted out by the use of circular queue.

Eg:

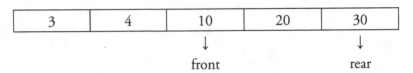

3	4	10	20	30
		↓		↓
		front		rear

In this case when we try to push an element, an error message will be printed stating that the queue is full. However, it can be easily seen that there are still empty spaces left in the array. This leads to a lot of wastage of the memory.

That is why we use circular queue. In this the rear end or the front end pointer reset to their initial location after they exceed the capacity of the queue.

Ques.14.11 Write a program to insert an element in a circular queue.

```java
import java.util.*;
class insert_operation
{
        public static void main (String[]args)
        {
                Scanner st = new Scanner (System.in);
                int q[] = new int [10];
                int size=10, n, f, r;
                int f = r = -1;
                System.out.println("enter the element to be inserted");
                n = st.nextInt();
                for (int x=1; x<10; x++)
                {
                        q[x] = 0;
                }
                if ((f == 0 && r == (size-1)) || f == r+1)
                {
                        System.out.println("QUEUE OVERFLOW");
                }
                else
                {
                        if (f == -1 && r == -1)
                        {
                                f = 0;
                                r = 0;
                        }
                        else
                        {
                                if ( r == size-1)
```

```
                    r = 0;
            else
                    r++;
        }
    q[r] = n;
        }
    }
}
```

Algorithm:

Step 1 - check for overflow
        if ((f = 0 and r = size-1) or f = r+1) then display
        "QUEUE OVERFLOW"
Step2 - set the pointers
        if (f == nul and r == null) then set f = 0 and r = 0
        else if (r = size) then set r = 0.
        else set r = r+1.
Step 3 - insert element
        queue[r] = item.

Ques.14.12 Write a program to delete an element from a circular queue.

```java
import java.util.*;
class delete_operation
{
        public static void main (String[]args)
        {
                Scanner st = new Scanner (System.in);
                int q[] = new int [10];
                int size=10, n, f, r;
                int f = r = -1;
                for (int x=1; x<10; x++)
                {
                        q[x] = 0;
                }
                if (f == -1 && r == -1)
                {
                        System.out.println("QUEUE UNDERFLOW");
```

```
        }
        else
        {
                n = q[f];
                if (f == size-1)
                {
                        f = 0;
                }
                else
                {
                if ( f == r)
                {
                        f = -1;
                        r = -1;
                }
                else
                f++;
                }
        }
    }
}
```

Algorithm:

Step1 - check for under flow
        if (f = null and r = null) then display "QUEUE UNDERFLOW"
Step 2 - delete an element
        value = queue[f]
Step 3 - set the pointers
        if (f = size) then set f = 0
        else if (f = r) then set f = null and r = null
        else set r = r+1

14.6 DEQUEUE

DQUEUE refers to double ended queue. It is similar simple queue except for the condition that insertion and deletion can be performed from both the ends of the queue.

Dequeue is classified into two types:
1) Input Restricted Dequeue
2) Output Restricted Dequeue

Ques 14.13 Write an algorithm to push an element at the rear end of the dequeue.

Step 1 - Start
Step 2 - Declare dq[] of maximum size N, r, f.
Step 3 - Assign r = -1 and f = -1
Step 4 - Accept limit of N
Step 5 - Check if r = N-1, then print "DEQUEUE OVERFLOW"; goto step 9 else goto step 6
Step 6 - Read an element
Step 7 - r++
Step 8 - Insert element, dq[r] = element
Step 9 - End

Ques 14.14 Write an algorithm to pop element from the front of dequeue of size N

Step 1 - Start
Step 2 - Assign r = N-1 and f = -1
Step 3 - Check if f>r then display "DEQUEUE UNDERFLOW", goto step 7 else goto step 4
Step 4 - While (f < = r), repeat steps 5 and 6.
Step 5 - f++
Step 6 - temp = dq[f]
Step 7 - End

Ques 14.15 Write an algorithm push an element at the front end of the dequeue

Step 1 - Start
Step 2 - Declare dq[] of maximum size N
Step 3 - Assign f = N-1
Step 4 - Check if f = 0 then print "DEQUEUE OVERFLOW", then go to step 8 else go to step 5.
Step 5 - Read an element

Step 6 - f--
Step 7 - Insert the element, dq[f] = element
Step 8 - End

Ques 14.16 Write an algorithm to pop an element from the rear end of the dequeue.

Step 1 - Start
Step 2 - Declare dq[] of maximum size N, r = N-1
Step 3 - Check if (f> r) or f = -1 or r = -1 then print "DEQUEUE
        UNDERFLOW", goto step 7 else goto step 4
Step 4 - While (f > = r), repeat steps 5 and 6.
Step 5 - temp = dq[r]
Step 6 - r --
Step 7 - End

14.7 QUESTION HOUR

(i)   What do you mean by data structure ?
(ii)   What is the meaning of FIFO and LIFO ?
(iii)   What is a stack ? Why is it used?
(iv)   Define Stack Overflow and Underflow.
(v)   What is a queue?
(vi)   Give one major drawback of a linear queue.
(vii)   What is the difference between circular queue and dequeue.
(viii) Define Queue Overflow and underflow.
(ix)   Can an array have two stacks ?
(x)   What is the use of queue ?
(xi)   Why are postfix and prefix expressions used ?
(xii)   Give the algorithm to convert an infix expression to a postfix
        expression.
(xiii) Give the algorithm to convert an infix expression to a prefix
        expression.

CHAPTER 15

LINKED LIST

Programs at a Glance

- Method to create a singly linked list containing N nodes. Print the linked list
- Method to count number of nodes present in a linked list.
- Method to insert a node at the beginning of a linked list.
- Method to insert an element in the middle of a linked list.
- Method to insert an element at the end of a linked list.
- Method to delete a node from a linked list
- Algorithm to search an element in a linked list
- Algorithm to merge the linked lists.
- Algorithm to split a linked list

15.1 INTRODUCTION

It is a structure based on the random arrangement of memory locations. It is a non linear structure that allows one to avail the facilities of storing data in random available empty spaces and linking them together in a way such that manipulation can be done as simply as in array.

Each element in the list is known as a node. IT contains to fields, data and link. The data field stores data while the address of the next list is stored in the link field.

Programming Examples

Ques 15.1 Write a method to create a singly linked list containing N nodes. Print the linked list

```
import java.io.*;
import java.util.*;
class node
{
        int data;
        node link;
        node()
        {
                data =0;
```

```
            link = null;
    }
    void create ()
    {
            int n;
            InputStreamReader read = new
            InputStreamReader(System.in);
            BufferedReader in = new BufferedReader(read);
            System.out.println("enter first data");
            this.data = Integer.parseInt(in.readLine());
            System.out.println("enter number of nodes");
            n = Integer.parseInt(in.readLine());
            node temp;
            node ptr = this;
            for (int x = 1; x<n; x++)
            {
                    temp=new node();
                    System.out.println("enter next data");
                    temp.data = Integer.parseInt(in.readLine());
                    temp.link = null;
                    ptr.link = temp;
                    temp = null;
                    ptr = ptr.link;
            }
    }
}
```

Algorithm :

Step 1 - Start

Step 2 - Declare pointer variables f, temp, m and other suitable variables

Step 3 - Read number of nodes to be created in N.

Step 4 - f = new node

Step 5 - Read list[f]

Step 6 - list[next] = null

Step 7 - temp = f

Step 8 - for i =1 to N-1, repeat Steps 7 to 13

Step 9 - m = new node

Step 10 - read list[m]

Step 11 - list[next] = null
Step 12 - temp[next] = m
Step 13 - temp = m
Step 14 - for i =1 to n, repeat step 15
Step 15 - display list[i]
Step 16 - End

Ques 15.2 Write an method to count number of nodes present in a linked list.

```
void countnode(node start)
{
      int c =0;
      node ptr = start;
      while ( ptr != null)
      {
            c++;
            ptr = ptr.link;
      }
      System.out.println("NO. of nodes in the list are = "+c);
}
```

Algorithm:

Step 1 - Start
Step 2 - Declare suitable pointer variable first.
Step 3 - Assign 0 to count
Step 4 - pointer = start
Step 5 - while (pointer != null), repeat steps 6 and 7
Step 6 - count++
Step 7 - pointer -> data, pointer = pointer->data.
Step 8 - Display "Number of nodes in the list", count
Step 9 - End

NOTE:- note the difference between START in step 1 which denotes the begining of the algorithm and START in step 4 where it denotes the head of the linked list.

Ques 15.3 Write an method to insert a node at the beginning of a linked list.

```
void insertbeg (node start, int x)
{
        node temp = new node();
        System.out.println("Enter element for new list");
        temp.data = x;
        temp.link = null;
        temp.link = start;
        start = temp;
        temp = null;
}
```

Algorithm :

Step 1 - Start
Step 2 - Declare suitable pointer variables
Step 3 - Check if linked list is empty then print "EMPTY LIST" go to step 7
Step 4 - Accept (temp -> data). temp -> link = null
Step 5 - temp-> link = start
Step 6 - start = temp. temp = null
Step 7 - End

Ques 15.4 Write a method to insert an element in the middle of a linked list.

```
void insertmid ( node start, int x, int n)
{
        node temp = new node();
        Syastem.out.println("enter new element for the list");
        temp.data = x;
        temp.link = null;
        node ptr = start;
        int c = 0;
```

```
    while (c<=n)
    {
            ptr = ptr.link;
            c++;
    }
    temp.link = ptr.link;
    ptr.link = temp;
}
```

Algorithm :

Step 1 - Start
Step 2 - Declare suitable pointer variables.
Step 3 - accept (temp->data). temp->link = null
Step 4 - ptr = start
Step 5 - count = 0
Step 6 - while (count < n), repeat steps 7 and8
Step 7 - ptr = ptr->link
Step 8 - count++
Step 9 - temp-> link = ptr->link. ptr->link = temp
Step 10 - temp = null. ptr = null.
Step 11 - End

Ques 15.5 Write a method to insert an element at the end of a linked list.

```
void insertend (node start, int x)
{
        node temp = new node();
        System.out.println("enter element for new list");
        temp.data = x;
        temp.link = null;
        node ptr = start;
        while (ptr.link !+ null)
        {
                ptr = ptr.link;
        }
        ptr.link = temp;
        temp = ptr = null;
}
```

Algorithm:

Step 1 - Start
Step 2 - Declare all the suitable pointer variables
Step 3 - Acccept (temp->data). temp->link = null
Step 4 - ptr = start
Step 5 - while(ptr->link != null), repeat step 6
Step 6 - ptr = ptr-> link
Step 7 - ptr->link = temp
Step 8 - ptr = null. temp = null
Step 9 - End

Ques 15.6 Write a method to delete a node from a linked list

```java
void delete(node start, int n)
{
        node ptr = start;
        node ptr1 = ptr;
        int c=0;
        while ( c<= n)
        {
                ptr1 = ptr;
                ptr = ptr.link;
                c++;
        }
        ptr1.link = ptr.link;
        ptr.link = null;
        ptr = ptr1 = null;
}
```

Algorithm :

Step 1 - Start
Step 2 - Declare the suitable pointer variables
Step 3 - ptr = start. ptr1 = start.
Step 4 - count =0
Step 5 - while (count<n) repeat the steps 6 to 8
Step 6 - ptr1 = ptr
Step 7 - ptr = ptr->link

Step 8 - count++
Step 9 - ptr1->link =ptr-> link
Step 10 - ptr->link = null
Step 11 - ptr = ptr1 = null
Step 12 - End

Ques 15.7 Write an algorithm to merge the linked lists

Step 1 - Start
Step 2 - ptr = start
Step 3 - while (ptr->link !+ null) repeat step 4
Step 4 - ptr = ptr->link
Step 5 - ptr->link = start1
Step 6 - ptr = null
Step 7 - End

NOTE:- Here in STEP 3 . . . we are locating the last node of the first link list. And in STEP 5 we are connecting the two link lists, where start1 is the head of the second link list

Ques 15.6 Write an algorithm to split a linked list

Step 1 - Start
Step 2 - ptr = start
Step 3 - count =0;
Step 4 - while(count<n), repeat the steps 5 and 6
Step 5 - ptr = ptr->link
Step 6 - count+
Step 7 - start1 = ptr->link.
Step 8 - ptr->link = null
Step 9 - End

NOTE:- here start1 denotes the head of the second link list. so that the first linked list would contain the elements before nth node and the second linked list would have elements after the nth node.